JEWELRY

in europe and america
new times, new thinking

RALPH TURNER

219 illustrations, 153 in colour

Thames and Hudson

This book is dedicated to Paul.
It is also in memory of my parents and John.

This book marks the occasion of the exhibition
Jewelry in Europe and America: New Times, New Thinking
and has been published in collaboration with the
Crafts Council of Great Britain.

Key to captions: C=circumference; Dia=diameter; H=height; L=length; W=width

© 1996 Thames and Hudson Ltd, London

British Library Cataloguing-in-Publication Data

A catalogue record for this book is available from the British Library

ISBN 0-500-27879-2

Printed and bound in Singapore by C.S. Graphics

CONTENTS

AUTHOR'S NOTE

In the pages of this book the reader will find names of many to whom I owe a debt of gratitude: Eugene Bielawski, Onno Boekhoudt, Caroline Broadhead, Joke Brakman, Alan Davie, Paul Derrez, Helen Drutt, Bob Ebendorf, Fritz Falk, Schmuckmuseum, Pforzheim, Arline Fisch, Toni Greenbaum, Patrick Heron, Hermann Jünger, Malcolm and Sue Knapp, Otto Künzli, Bruno and Carla Martinazzi, Bruce Metcalf, Robert Lee Morris, Louis Mueller, Gian Carlo Montebello, Francesco Pavan, Ronald Pearson, Arnaldo Pomodoro, Jack Prip, Dorothea Prühl, Louise Smit, Rachelle Thiewes and Graziano Visintin.

I would also like to thank those who are not mentioned yet who have given me their time and encouragement: Sarah Bodine; Susan Cummins; Liesbeth Crommlin, Stedilijk Museum, Amsterdam; Richard Edgcumbe, Victoria and Albert Museum, London; Daphne Farago; Jeanine Falino, Boston Museum of Fine Arts; Graziella Falchini Grassetto; John Grant; Richard Hollis; Rudiger Joppien, Museum für Kunst und Gewerbe, Hamburg; Yvonne Joris, Museum Het Kruithuis, 's Hertogenbosch; Carin Delcourt van Krimpen; Kieron Kramer; Charon Kransen; David McFadden, Cooper-Hewitt Museum, New York; Valerie Mitchell; Luc d'Iberville Moreau, Musée des Arts Décoratifs, Montreal; Susan Mossman, The Science Museum, London; Michael Munroe, Renwick Gallery, Smithsonian Institution, Washington; Greg Nacozy; Peter Nickl; Eunice and Tod Pardon; Berend Peters; Michael Pinnock; Michael Rowe, Royal College of Art, London; Rosemary Ransome-Wallis, Worshipful Company of Goldsmiths, Goldsmiths Hall, London; Helen Shirk; Linda Theophilus; Kenneth Trapp, Oakland Museum of California; Scott Vanderham, American Crafts Museum, New York.

Finally I would like to thank Alison Jenkins, the staff of the Crafts Council, Thames and Hudson and two friends: Jenni Spencer-Davies and Paul McAlinden whose encouragement and support made the project possible.

INTRODUCTION

My initial encounter with artist jewelry came about in the sixties when I was a young actor. During one of my all-too-frequent 'resting' periods I took a job and drifted into the art world under the wings of Ewan Phillips, the English art historian, and Kathleen Grant, who was a jeweler. As an assistant in their London gallery, my eyes and mind began to open to a new world of modern painting and sculpture. With the zeal of the convert I fed ferociously on modern art, absorbing it night and day at a rate of knots.

As for jewelry, I had never really given it much thought save to ogle occasionally and gawp at the gewgaws in jewelry shops. But the work we showed in the gallery was unlike anything I had seen before. Some jewelry was theatrical, bold, brave, even and exciting. Some artists' work was more confrontational, striking out at conformity with uncompromising designs. As my interest in modern jewelry developed alongside my understanding of painting and sculpture, I began to realise that there was more to the jeweler's art than marvellous, expensive artifice. I was hooked. This was how I cut my teeth on artist jewelry – the subject of this survey.

This book follows the same innovative spirit of jewelry in America and Europe – namely Britain, Germany, Holland and Italy. It charts the development of the pioneering careers that have informed studio jewelry's evolution from the 1940s to the present day. Attention is largely focused on work that challenges conventions and on ideas that often go beyond traditional notions of personal adornment.

The idea for the book emerged out of my work for an exhibition at the Crafts Council in London, both taking almost two years to research and write. The project involved travelling to places that are as remote from each other spiritually as they are geographically. The account I present, therefore, is a personal and subjective selection of work I consider to have been seminal in the development of jewelry in the last fifty years.

The scope of both the exhibition and the book is ambitious and there are inevitable omissions due to unavoidable limitations of time and space. The 1980s, for example, are introduced only summarily as this period is covered in depth in my last book, co-authored with Peter Dormer and revised in 1994, *The New Jewelry: Trends and Traditions*, first published by Thames and Hudson in 1985.

Studio jewelry is a term now frequently used to distinguish the work of artists from work produced purely for commerical reasons. This kind of distinction can be traced back to the Arts and Crafts movement in rural Victorian England, although its application to jewelry properly began in mid-20th-century New York, amidst its 'canyons of steel'.

The lack of goldsmithing traditions in the United States meant that jewelry there developed in a polarized way that was independent from activity in Europe (there had always been an exchange of influences between European countries). This relative isolation in the US prompted individual innovation which in the 1940s and 1950s aligned itself with Surrealism, Constructivism and Primitivism. However, when in the

1970s American design in studio jewelry was growing with confidence and developing its own unique aesthetic, an unexpected European influence began to emerge.

In Europe, the post-war recovery was slow, impeding jewelry's progress. It was not until the 1960s that things really started to improve, when increasing affluence and greater social equality gave rise to higher education for more people. The rapid growth in the number of art schools saw a new generation bringing fresh ideas to expand the boundaries of modern jewelry with new, colourful and sometimes controversial expressions.

Traditions on both sides of the Atlantic were challenged, including the long-held perception that women wear expensive jewelry as a symbol of the wealth of the man to whom they 'belong'. This, of course, was seen as both sexist and elitist, an attitude that still muddies the waters for many studio jewelers who strongly refute its continuing contamination. The questioning of the status of precious jewelry has resulted in inventive alternatives and original designs being made from new and unlikely materials. Now that stylistic allegiances are less certain, new causes are found. Eclectic rummaging through symbolism, mythology, metaphor and ethnic cultures run parallel to conceptual idioms; traditional materials and techniques are making a comeback in jewelry, performances and installation-based work. Undiluted sensual and sexual interpretation of jewelry has also increased as makers explore the body as a territory for uninhibited expression.

With a growing international awareness and an ever-increasing vocabulary, artist jewelry today monitors social change. This provides a socially viable role for the jewelers in a medium which is as exciting to practise as it is to observe.

CHAPTER I

AMERICA 1940–1980

CREATING AN IDENTITY

Throughout the 20th century, America's competitive spirit romped through the modern world challenging the old world's sensitivities. With youthful exuberance it liberated itself from its parental roots – particularly the European ones. This emancipation did not happen overnight, but grew with confidence after World War II, almost two hundred years after America's independence from Britain.

From the 1930s onwards, artistic life in America grew rapidly as European refugees fled from the horrors of Fascism and Nazism. New York especially attracted artists, and as the new arrivals were absorbed into its fabric, the centre of the art world was transported there from Paris.

Yet despite this influx from the European avant-garde, American studio jewelry largely developed independently of European goldsmithing traditions. And, apart from the American Indian culture, North America had no traditions of indigenous goldsmithing influences, thus enabling a handful of pioneering artists to explore the language of jewelry more freely. New York, where Sam Kramer and Art (Arthur) Smith were important influences, was the centre of this activity during and after the war.

Sam Kramer's shop on Eighth Street became the haunt in the 1940s and 1950s for those in search of psychic fantasy. In place of the usual ordered display, his jewelry outlet was untidy and exotic. Skulls, shells, petrified wood and geological specimens crowded the interior (he had studied geology at New York University). The silversmith John Prip recalls: 'It seemed to be open 24 hours a day and was a place to linger and listen to village gossip as Sam tinkered away at the back.' Arline Fisch describes the shop's likeness in the 1950s to 'Edward Kienholz's "Beanery" installation – colourful and exotic.' Kramer was considered an eccentric even by New York's standards. He plundered the subconscious for Surrealist images that opposed the Modernist spirit of the time, considering modern designs cold and sterile. For the neatly costumed figures of the 1940s, his jewelry was considered outrageous. 'Things to titillate the damnest ego – utter weirdities conceived in moments of semi-madness . . . ' hailed Kramer's advertising flyer. With teeth, taxidermic eyes and meteorites, Kramer created fiendish, witty fantasies for his clients, who in later years included Beats, Rockers and Hippies. They must have worshipped him.

Racial prejudice was still widespread in America during the 1940s and 1950s. In 1946, Art Smith, a black American jeweler, opened his own business in New York's Little Italy, but was forced to move to a more liberal location on West Fourth Street. Customers would drop into his Greenwich Village shop, enticed inside by Duke Ellington on the gramophone. Music, and particularly dance, were a motivating force in Smith's jewelry; he designed large-scale pieces for black dance companies. His visual vocabulary emphasized his fascination with African biomorphism, which he used to explore his own sensuality. Jewelry's relationship to the human form was central to his thinking. 'A piece of jewelry,' he said, 'is a "what is it?" until you relate it to the body.'

Sam and Carol Kramer at home in New York, *c.* 1947

The spiral forms of Art Smith's work might owe something to the fertile imagination of the American sculptor, Alexander Calder. Like several fine artists of his generation, Calder also made jewelry; but, unlike most, his contribution was significant, devoting whole exhibitions to the subject at the Willard Gallery in New York in the 1940s. It is unlikely that Smith would have missed these new interpretations of neo-Primitivism. Calder's materials were usually modest: often bent and beaten wire made of brass, copper or iron, and occasionally silver and gold. The results were monumental in scale, sometimes reminiscent of African, Greek and other ethnic jewelry.

Calder's working methods were simple and were taken up by many would-be jewelers as they seized hammer and wire to follow suit. But there were also more subtle interpretations, such as those of Smith and Harry Bertoia. Bertoia was mainly a product designer who worked with Charles and Ray Eames in California and, later, Knoll Associates in Pennsylvania. Bertoia's modern classic chickenwire Diamond chair, designed for Knoll in 1952, is still, happily, in production. Its aesthetic, however, is far removed from his hand-wrought Calderesque jewelry. Bertoia was also a teacher at the famous Cranbrook Academy of Art in Michigan, where he became a mentor for the younger generation. His influence was also acknowledged by Earl Pardon, who was to become an important figure in studio jewelry. Pardon's work in the 1950s epitomized the spatial use of materials at that time with fluid structures capturing the spirit of Modernism. Early recognition of his jewelry came in 1954 with a two-person exhibition in Detroit with the painter Josef Albers.

In 1940, at a summer school in Oakland, California, Margaret de Patta, a 37-year-old jeweler from Tacoma, met the artist László Moholy-Nagy. The following year, she enrolled at his School of Design in Chicago, which he funded himself, directing a modified and up-dated version of Bauhaus principles. Just as he had done in Germany, Moholy-Nagy spread ideas and utopian concepts to talented pupils. 'Catch your stones in the air . . . make them float in space. Don't enclose them,' he told her.

Energized by his teaching, de Patta evolved a series of jewelry pieces with open, lightweight metalwork constructions and transparent stones, uniquely cut to manipulate the light. Soon, however, she was unable to meet the demand for this one-off, time-consuming work and set up a limited production range, which she organized with her husband, the designer Eugene Bielawski. Philanthropy played a part in this, with de Patta feeling socially and philosophically motivated to bring her Modernist jewelry within the reach of a wider public. Production pieces sold for under $50, but despite its success, marketing became burdensome and overwhelming, and the production ceased. De Patta's interpretation of Constructivism elevated both her own work and American jewelry's niche in the history of 20th-century art.

The work of other Constructivists affected the designs of studio jewelry in America during the 1940s and 1950s. Irena Brynner acknowledges the influence of Vladimir Tatlin for her spiral jewelry, and Ed Wiener drew considerable inspiration from the Cubist style of Alexander Archipenko. Interestingly, Wiener's most famous jewel was a stylistic interpretation of a photograph taken in 1941 by Barbara Morgan of Martha Graham dancing. So popular was Wiener's brooch, which he made in 1948, that 100 copies were produced. Many were sold to dancers from his West 53rd Street shop, well placed to attract New York's culturati, being next to MOMA.

When the war ended, a pessimistic and disillusioned generation turned to the crafts as an alternative way of life. Often with little or no formal training, their improvised skills steered American jewelry towards unorthodox methods. Uninhibited by formal teaching, a 'make-do' aesthetic developed. Coincidentally, the US Military set up a rehabilitation programme to train young ex-servicemen in craft skills for their return to civvy street.

In contrast to these somewhat amateurish *ad hoc* arrangements, two American goldsmiths craved the dexterity of virtuosos. One was Margret Craver from Boston, an influential teacher and early pioneer of American studio jewelry. With patience she revitalized the lost 16th-century enamelling process, *en résille*. The other was John Paul Miller from Ohio, who rediscovered the ancient Etruscan technique of granulation – the art of embellishing a surface with vast numbers of infinitesimally small spheres of gold. Both Craver's classical restraint and Miller's zoomorphic creations brought to American jewelry a scholarship that is now recognized internationally.

Official recognition of contemporary American crafts came as early as 1939 with the formation of the American Crafts Council. (In Britain, the Crafts Advisory Committee, later the Crafts Council, was founded in 1971.) By 1946, aesthetic standards in American jewelry prompted the Museum of Modern Art to attempt to dismantle the boundaries separating the fine and applied arts by staging a large exhibition, 'Modern Jewelry Design'. It presented 'a new concept in jewelry: wearable art'. This exhibition brought to New York's attention the philosophy of the wearable,

Margaret de Patta at home in San Francisco with photographer Romeo Rolette, 1942

modern, 'miniature sculpture' in which the values of the materials were subordinate to the ideas. Throughout the 1950s, the spirit of Modernism in America spread through other innovative designers, such as Paul Lobel, Philip Morton, Merry Renk and Bob Winston. By the end of the decade, abstract Modernist designs were widespread with many workshops churning out repetitive and imitative work. However, notwithstanding MOMA's initiative, separation between the arts continued.

AMERICAN TRANSFORMATIONS

Along with their permissiveness, the 1960s will be remembered as a period of expansion with a growth in the number of universities and art schools, bringing higher education within the reach of more people. This broader cultural and ethnic mix brought with it greater radical expectations from education. In the late 1960s, students in America and Europe rebelled against the narrowness of curricula and the stifling effects of authoritarianism in society. This eventually generated a more diversified curriculum with a more liberal approach.

Arline Fisch, from San Diego, was one who at that heady time championed jewelry's cause and its creative potential through her work and in education. She questioned the accepted definition of jewelry by exploring, with large-scale body pieces, the boundaries between sculpture and personal ornament. These broke with the tradition of well-mannered, discreet decoration. Fisch is also known for her inventive adaptations in metal of knitting techniques and for introducing them into jewelry. Her career now represents a cornerstone in jewelry's recent history, not least through her teaching and her energetic promotion of American work abroad. Marjorie Schick is also a pioneer of body works with spectacular experiments that hovered on the brink of function. Her powerful work in the 1960s preceded most other experiments on both sides of the Atlantic by almost a decade. Schick's uninhibited investigations continue today, but the wooden body constructions are now larger, more colourful and decorative.

The emergence of Pop art in the late 1950s and early 1960s, although born in England, was embraced in America and had an instant appeal for young people, not least jewelers, who adopted its bright and subversive character. With wit and intelligence, Fred Woell's work exploded upon American jewelry, exposing its latent revolutionary spirit. Abandoning his former reductivist style along with most precious metals, Woell turned to using popular American icons as symbols for his Pop messages. Found objects, photography, advertising, packaging and other ephemera found their way into his collages. (Such calculated shock value had been applied to jewelry earlier by Dada and Surrealist artists, such as Man Ray and Hans Arp.) These essays by Woell were heroic and nostalgic, but the strength and conviction of his work drove out any possible signs of sentimentality.

ARLINE FISCH
Body ornament worn by the artist, 1967
Repoussé and chased sterling silver.
H 114 cm
American Crafts Museum, New York

In 1968 in Chicago, jeweler, teacher and author Philip Morton called together fellow goldsmiths to form a support group, the members of which became the founders of the Society of North American Goldsmiths. SNAG represented, at that time, many of the trail-blazers of the jewelry and metalwork avant-garde: Robert Ebendorf, Phillip Fike, Hero Kielman, Barrie Kington, Stanley Lechtzin, Kurt Matzdorf, Ronald Pearson and Olaf Skoogfors. Their aims were ambitious – to achieve recognition by the fine art world in the new decade.

Robert Ebendorf, attracted to the new, was initially drawn to Pop art, adapting its colourful, figurative aesthetic; he later chose a more conceptual path of investigation, to which I will return later. Olaf Skoogfors was born in Sweden but emigrated to the USA as a child. He travelled widely and his enthusiasm for German work and, perhaps more importantly, Swedish influences, was infectious and can be detected in his sensitive approach. The cool, reductionist logic of Scandinavian design found other converts in American jewelry, among them Ronald Pearson and John Prip. In 1952, in Rochester, they joined with other craftspeople to form Shop One, a cooperative promoting fine crafts. Its aesthetic drew on Prip's Danish background and utilized Pearson's entrepreneurial talent.

Robert Ebendorf, 1960

Stanley Lechtzin, another founder of SNAG, is regarded by his peers as a kind of wizard. Keeping a steely eye on the latest technological developments, he created jewelry that would have been impossible without industrial methods. In the 1960s, he adapted electroforming techniques that enabled him to make large-scale, feather-light work in gold and silver. Throughout the 1970s, these developed into elephantine torques, pendants and brooches intimidating all but the most self-assured wearer. As larger and larger jewelry found its way into exhibitions and magazines, this prompted rivalry amongst some American goldsmiths, notably Richard Mawdsley, whose mechanistic, tubular constructions are often referred to as icons of fantasy. Currently, Lechtzin's working methods are computer-led, from design stage to production. At the Tyler School of Art in Philadelphia, Lechtzin's students have access to an impressive electroforming laboratory with CAD/CAM facilities.

Another American virtuoso who studied at Tyler was Albert Paley, whose assertive interpretations of jewelry raised eyebrows around the world, although he is better known today for his massive ornamental ironworks. He acknowledges Lechtzin's 'profound, demanding but professional influence.' His pieces, like his architectural commissions, are not intended as mere adornment, but are very much regarded by him as sculpture: both for buildings and for the human body, in particular the female body. While he was, of course, not alone in this ambition in the 1970s, Paley challenged the European vanguard more than any other American jeweler. He helped to build an American aesthetic, despite his swaggering interpretations of art nouveau.

13

above
ALBERT PALEY
Pendant, 1974
Formed and fabricated silver, Delrin, copper.
H 49 cm

above centre
Albert Paley on his bench commissioned by
the Victoria and Albert Museum, 1994
Forged iron, mahogany. W 343 cm

above far right
Claus Bury in Hanau, Germany, 1975

Such monumental jewelry, with its overt sensuality and sexual overtones, can make demands on the wearer. I asked Paley who would expose themselves to this situation. 'Strong women with strong personalities,' he said. Artists claim these demands are a prerequisite and that social and behavioural adjustments are integral to the concept of their work. I will return to this moot topic, which is so prevalent in modern jewelry.

Until the 1970s, jewelry in the USA had developed largely in a polarized way. The work was often larger, louder and, some might say, freer than in Europe. From a European perspective, the work was thought wildly extravagant, with a strange amalgam of incomprehensible styles. But things were to change.

In 1973, Claus Bury, a 27-year-old jeweler from Hanau, visited the USA for the first time. The previous year he had won a coveted award at the International Jewelry Competition at Germany's Schmuckmuseum (Jewelry Museum) in Pforzheim. Toni Greenbaum, an American author and jewelry historian in New York, writes:

> *Bury's visit proved to be a watershed; his inventive use of bonded acrylic and metal in mechanistic 'landscapes', along with his applications of jewelry as one element in a sculpture or diagram, altered the course of American jewelry history, away from the ornamental towards the conceptual.*

Bury's talent and assertive personality took hold of America. Robert Ebendorf was an early convert. His own work changed directions, adopting a more conceptual approach. Jill Slosburg-Ackerman was also a devotee of Bury. Her early work translated natural forms in repetitive, organic structures into jewelry and sculptural installations that had a close similarity. Both Slosburg-Ackerman and Ebendorf held senior teaching positions at the Massachusetts College of Art in Boston and the State University of New York at New Paltz, respectively, thus continuing Bury's influence and enabling his work to be widely interpreted. He had introduced to American jewelry not only a new visual aesthetic, but also a new rigorous attitude to working.

left
JILL SLOSBURG-ACKERMAN
L'Eau Relief (detail), 1977
Papier-mâché, steel. H 15 cm;
floor space 336 x 305 cm

above
JILL SLOSBURG-ACKERMAN
Brooch, 1975
Sterling silver. W 11.4 cm

After Bury's visit to the USA came Hermann Jünger and his refined, cultivated aesthetic and a humanity which deeply impressed all who came into contact with him and his work. With evangelical zeal, the European cultural stream swelled into a flood: Friedrich Becker, Gijs Bakker, Emmy van Leersum, Wendy Ramshaw, David Watkins and many other European goldsmiths crossed the Atlantic in the 1970s, some with trepidation, but all with the dedication and vocation of missionaries.

Not everyone, however, in America had been waiting for, or was in need of, this youthful influx of new ideas from Europe. There was an endemic American aesthetic developing from its historical diversity of styles and excessive interpretation of ornament that bore little relationship to European sensibilities. Ken Cory had already explored the status issue surrounding jewelry in the 1960s with his refined graphic work dissociated from precious materials. His pieces, which dealt consistently with sculptural concerns, were noted for their visual sharpness and for never losing sight of jewelry's function: that it is to be worn. Barry Merritt, in the early 1970s, was obsessed with Funk jewelry. He was an early convert to Body art, which flaunted fetishism and addressed women's sexuality. Merritt would have been unlikely to cool his ardour to acquire a less spicy European aesthetic. William Harper's anthropomorphic interpretations – potent, fetishistic and erotic – emblazoned his iconographic enamel work. Thomas Gentille in New York is another, though quite different, example of an American whose thorough intellectual investigations and interpretations of materials and techniques were unaffected by European goldsmithing influences. His preoccupation looks elsewhere. His deep interest in ancient cultures has influenced the forms in his work while he has adapted a Japanese lacquering technique traditionally used for screens and furniture. This invention uses pure pigment and eggshell – a secret process he strongly guards. Yet his cool, Modernist aesthetic was a precursor of future developments. Although many artists in the US were impressed with European work – among them Lechtzin, Woell, Paley, Schick and Fisch – they continued to develop an independent tradition of American jewelry.

KEN CORY
Tongue, brooch, 1967
Silver, leather, stone. H 7 cm

CHAPTER II

EUROPE 1945–1970: RECOVERY AND RECONSTRUCTION

When American culture was limbering up the scales with its pluralistic voice, Europe was holding its breath. In 1945, at the end of World War II, Europe was battered, exhausted and changed, with the arts, like so much else, affected by the austerity that came to dominate people's lives.

Consumerism in America, on the other hand, flourished, offering its superficial fix for a happy life. Its all-pervasive tentacles soon spread to Europe, which first learned of its delights vicariously through the cinema and television. A growing number of people in Europe, as in America, chose to distance themselves from this antiseptic, air-wick culture and turned to the crafts as a cure for contemporary ills. Pottery, textiles and furniture-making were popular for those with 'back-to-the-land' dispositions, while jewelry remained largely an urban activity – close to ideas, materials and clients.

Europe has a distinguished goldsmithing ancestry, unlike America. However, its history has not always been seen as enabling: some artists find it inhibiting, stultifying creative thinking. Jewelry's alignment with commerce and fashion has also been viewed as suspicious and sometimes debilitating, at least in Britain.

BRITAIN

Unlike the rest of Europe, jewelry in Britain lies somewhat uncomfortably in the crafts community. William Morris, who founded the Arts and Crafts movement in Victorian England, set the highest standards for utilitarian goods but largely by-passed jewelry design. Jewelry's chief practitioner in the Arts and Crafts movement was Henry Wilson, whose formidable talent tended to emphasize the ailments of most other British goldsmiths at the time. Even the jewelry of C. R. Ashbee was reticent and over-refined. His heart and genius were somewhere else, amidst his houses, furniture and books. Perhaps jewelry's closeness to commerce was incompatible with Morris's socialist principles, as was the 'mere prettiness' of jewelry's fashion orientation for Ashbee.

With neither a 'father' nor 'mother' figure in British jewelry comparable in status to Bernard Leach in pottery or Ethel Mairet in weaving, the resurgence of the artist-jeweler developed slowly in post-war Britain. In the early 1950s, Britain was in the doldrums – rationing and austerity dampened the environment with drab, faded pre-war colours. The Festival of Britain, held in 1951, was intended as a morale-boosting exercise, with its 'tonic to the nation' flying the flag for contemporary design. Jewelry, however, was unimaginative and ultra-conservative.

Alan Davie, the British painter, made jewelry in the 1940s and 1950s to supplement his income. He had learned the rudiments of the craft at the Edinburgh School of Art and had developed a spiritual and symbolic style. His jewelry caught the attention of a public hungry for his interpretations of neo-Primitivism. Among his admirers was William Johnson, who, as Head of London's Central School of Art and Crafts, invited Davie, along with other painters, to enliven the school's basic design

ALAN DAVIE
Ring, c. 1958
Silver. H 4 cm
Victoria and Albert Museum, London

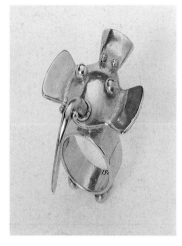

course. Victor Pasmore, Mary Kessel, Patrick Heron, Eduardo Paolozzi and Richard Hamilton were among the artistic recruits.

Gerda Flöckinger was a student at Central at about this time and well remembers the school buzzing with this new energy. Orthodox teaching methods were often given over to improvisation, for, as Davie recalls, 'Like most of the other artists who taught design at the Central, I was often learning just ahead of the students.'

On a trip to Rome in 1953, Gerda Flöckinger saw the jewelry of two Italian painters, Afro (Basaldella) and Lucio Fontana. She was deeply impressed and energized. That year she started to make her own jewelry: largely abstract silver and enamel compositions interpreting modernity in low relief. In the 1960s she abandoned this style and began fusing metals into flourishing abstract compositions. These generous swirling curves were textured with filigree and set with cabochon stones as pools of colour. This technique has seen little change over the years, yet its refinement continues to enthral. She achieved the distinction of being the first woman to hold a solo exhibition at the Victoria and Albert Museum in London, in 1971. In fact London ten years earlier, in 1961, proved to be a watershed for British jewelry. Under the artistic direction of Graham Hughes, the Goldsmiths Hall staged the 'International Exhibition of Modern Jewelry, 1890–1961', the first of its kind. In addition to Davie and Flöckinger were other British designers developing their work and careers: Gerald Benny, E. R. Nele, Andrew Grima, Rod Edwards, John Grenville, Louis Osman, Desmond Clen-Murphy, John Donald and Ernest Blythe.

Despite such burgeoning talents, Hughes felt the need to enliven the British contemporary section and commissioned sculptors and painters to make some pieces for the show. For Elizabeth Frink, Terry Frost, Merlyn Evans, Mary Kessel, Lynn Chadwick, Michael Ayrton, Kenneth Armitage, Robert Adams and William Scott, this was often their first and only experience of the crafts. Patrick Heron recalls a large lump of wax dropping through the letter box with an invitation from the Goldsmith's Hall inviting him to make something, but he declined, thinking it presumptuous to assume that painters could just make jewelry at the drop of a hat.

Britain's contribution to this exhibition also included work from Ukrainian-born Naum Slutzky, who had taught at the Bauhaus and who had emigrated to England in 1932. In the 1930s, his Modernist jewelry, even by Bauhaus standards, was light years ahead of its time. At the time of the exhibition, Slutzky was sixty-seven, with little sign of having relaxed his original Modernist principles.

With the expansion of British art education in the 1960s, more art schools offered a wider range of art and craft practices. Modern art, especially Pop art, made its greatest impact on young people, by-passing the middle aged and side-stepping the middle classes. Socially, the barriers were coming down, or were at least being

GERDA FLÖCKINGER
The artist wearing three of her rings, 1968
Silver, gold, pearls. H as shown 5 cm

Slutzky Again by Ronald Pennell, 1974
Ink on paper

17

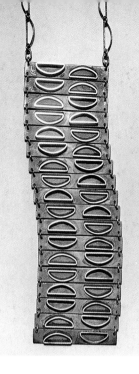

PATRICIA MEYEROWITZ
Pendant and chain, 1962
Silver. H 15.5 cm

Helga Zahn at home in London, 1976

relocated – a greater affluence blurred class distinctions, although a noticeable gap was beginning to grow between the generations.

Along with these developments, British jewelry began to shed some of its conservatism. It broadened the techniques used in studio jewelry and opened up new, less formal possibilities for design. Ewan Phillips opened his small gallery in London's Maddox Street in 1964. He exhibited fine works by modern painters and sculpture by his friends Leon Underwood and Henry Moore. Phillips's eclectic taste filled showcases with Roman glass, Pre-Columbian pottery, Asante weights, Ghandra-Buddhas and jewelry by fifty or so contemporary artists. This wide embrace of the arts was also my own education and introduction to the art world as a gallery assistant. Exhibitions were given to young painters and sculptors and also jewelers, including Gijs Bakker and Emmy van Leersum, providing them with their first exposure outside Holland. Other less maverick British jewelers included Catherine Mannheim, Peter Hauffé and Breon O'Casey, who, as a child, had been taught at Dartington by Slutzky. Round about this time, Patricia Meyerowitz was writing her first book on jewelry and sculpture, outlining her methods of compiling compound units, which she recycled into restrained, Constructivist work.

Helga Zahn was also an important liberating force in Britain at that time; she was a printmaker whose graphic images were sometimes reflected in her jewelry. She often complained of the time-consuming process of goldsmithing and its debilitating effect on spontaneity, but she was never one to compromise, not least with the scale of her formidable work.

GERMANY

Germany's recovery after the war was fraught by its partition: in the east, the German Democratic Republic became the puppet state of the USSR, leaving the west to form the Federal Republic of Germany. The Berlin Wall, built in 1961 by the East German Government to prevent mass emigration, was to become a symbol of oppression that lasted for almost thirty years.

West German culture, unlike its eastern counterpart, was given a boost in an effort to rebuild its existing traditions. Art schools and specialist institutions in goldsmithing opened again, forging new standards in technical prowess and creativity.

The most influential art school of the 20th century was of course the Bauhaus with its 1920s origins steeped in the Arts and Crafts movement. Its unifying focus was on craft subjects, which became an immense creative force, forming the essence of the modern movement. Its influence is alive today.

Friedrich Becker is recognized internationally as a pioneer of modern jewelry, yet few publications mention the parallels between his design in the 1950s and 1960s and the Bauhaus philosophy. Becker's championing of stark simplicity and functionalism

was also central to his thinking. With a background in aeronautical engineering, he contrived clever, inventive solutions that dispensed with orthodox stone settings – 'Catching the stones in the air', as Moholy-Nagy would have it. Becker's work in the 1960s was for a while in step with the cutting edge of contemporary sculpture. With cool Minimalism and breathtaking technique, he composed kinetic jewelry: the components – rotating disks, bars, cones and circles – were activated at astonishing speed by gravity and the wearer's movements.

Alongside Becker, there were three other key figures in the 1950s and 1960s who became chiefly responsible for securing the high standards of creativity in German jewelry: Reinhold Reiling, Klaus Ullrich and Hermann Jünger. Reiling was a goldsmith and a charismatic teacher with Ullrich at the Fachhochschule für Gestaltung at Pforzheim. His vision, which he shared with Karl Schollmayer, author and director of this influential school, was the resurgence of the jeweler as a free artist. Former students recall Reiling's energy, contagious enthusiasm and unstinting generosity in his teaching methods. Claus Bury, Jens-Rudiger Lorenzen, Onno Boekhoudt and Manfred Bischoff are disparate examples of Reiling's commitment to individualism. Reiling's own work was largely a mixture of influences from painting, mostly Abstract Expressionism and, later, Pop art. A few years before his death, however, he adopted a more reductivist approach.

Pforzheim is a small town near the Black Forest and since the 18th century it has been recognized as a centre of goldsmithing. During the Second World War, its many workshops were impounded and work in the town was given over to the manufacture of tiny component parts for bombs and armaments. The town itself was all but obliterated in the subsequent air raids, but was largely rebuilt during the fifties. The Schmuckmuseum was conceived in the early 1960s and is the only museum in the world devoted to the history of jewelry, tracing its development from early traditions to present-day techniques and styles. With its unique international collection and exhibitions programme directed by Fritz Falk, it continues to be a place of pilgrimage.

Munich also has a distinguished goldsmithing tradition which emphasizes the importance of contemporary jewelry, reinforced by the status of the Academy of Art, where Hermann Jünger taught from 1972 to 1990. Jünger was born in Hanau, near Frankfurt, in 1928 and opened his first studio there two years after the end of the

FRIEDRICH BECKER
Rings
(from left to right) Gold, rutilated quartz, 1957.
Gold, rose quartz and hematite, 1962.
Two white gold, kinetic rings shown in movement, 1971. H 3.9 cm

HERMANN JÜNGER
Necklace, 1957
Gold. L of pendants 7 cm
Museum für Kunst und Gewerbe, Hamburg

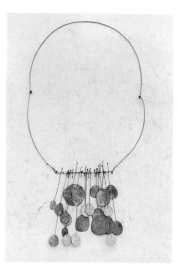

RENATE HEINTZE
Necklace, 1967
Silver, brass, agate. H 30 cm
Staatliche Museen, Berlin

Second World War. As a young goldsmith, his jewelry in the late 1950s was unlike any other. Distinctive, with a visual eloquence, its graphic, abstract imagery toyed with informality. Fastenings, for example, were made visible and impishly simple. The goldsmith's mark (normally concealed) sometimes became an integral part of the design. With a painter's eye, colour and balance punctuated subtle organic forms in necklaces and brooches that still reverberate with energy and beauty almost forty years after they were made.

There is a lucidity and freedom about Jünger's work. Juxtaposed with the heavy, mid-European design of his contemporaries, his light, airy work in precious metals looked refreshingly accessible. He is also a fine draughtsman and painter of expressive watercolours. With a sense of awe, I discovered that he designed some jewels by selecting the shapes formed from drips from his brush. The freedom that pervades his work contributes to its spontaneity, an elusive quality that, as Helga Zahn recalled, is hard to capture in the painstaking, lengthy process of goldsmithing. Of the individualists in German teaching, Jünger perhaps has been the most influential, being instrumental in nurturing so much young talent. Throughout the 1970s and 1980s, his work and personality dominated goldsmithing in Germany and continue to have a far-reaching influence abroad.

Halle is an industrial district that lies between Weimar and Dessau, homes of the Bauhaus in former East Germany. Amidst heavy industrial pollution, which makes the air reek with brown sulphurous fumes, an art school has taken refuge and nestles protected behind the confines of an ancient castellated fortification. In the 1950s and 1960s, jewelry at the Hochschule für Kunst und Design (High School of Art and Design) in Halle was dominated by the effects of Marxist Socialist thinking, with jewelry seen as 'an expression of feminine desire for ornament' and as a commodity that should be mass produced.

Dorothea Prühl, who now runs the course, told me that this somewhat patronizing, sexist attitude, with its emphasis on strict design ethics, then produced 'cold and impersonal jewelry devoid of colour, humour or sensuality.' Renate Heintze took over the jewelry department in the 1960s and championed a more liberal approach. 'Her energy and vision rushed through the school, suddenly there was excitement and so much to do,' Prühl recalls. The stimulus for this new approach may have come from outside, perhaps from Czechoslovakia, the reason being that prior to the reunification of Germany, travel outside the GDR had been restricted to countries within the Eastern Block. As Czechoslovakia's more liberal democratic tradition was for some time tolerated by the Soviets, its culture was considerably more open. Jewelry in particular was advanced, with artists of the calibre of Anton Cepka,

Svatopluk Kasally and Alena Nováková, whose work was on a par with developments in the West. Furthermore, the international jewelry exhibitions and symposia in Jablonec were unique opportunities to see work from other countries and to exchange ideas. All this came to an abrupt end in 1968 when Russian tanks invaded Prague.

HOLLAND

After the war, the Dutch Protestant ethic, with its characteristic efficiency and stoicism, regenerated the Netherlands, rebuilding its battered cities. In Rotterdam, Marcel Breuer designed one of his most important public buildings, the department store, De Bijenkorf, for which Naum Gabo was commissioned to create a large Constructivist sculpture in 1956. Its vast steel trunk emerged from the pavement with branches rising to a height of over 25 metres. Onno Boekhoudt, former Professor of Jewelry at the Rietveld Academy, remembers as a child noticing the abstract sculpture's impact on pedestrians and the excitement it generated. He believes that Gabo's futuristic work might have stimulated Dutch goldsmiths, for example, Archibald Dunbar, Chris Steenbergen and Ab Wouters, all of whom used elements of Constructivism in jewelry at that time.

The linear spiral and strung forms of Gabo and other Constructivists, such as Antoine Pevsner and Vladimir Tatlin, became important influences on Modernist jewelers in the mid-century, both in America and Europe. Such influences could be detected in Karl Niehouster's work in the late 1950s with its curvilinear elements repeating shapes and rhythms. There was also the importance of carving in many jewelers' work associated with honest, physical labour evoking the virtues of craftsmanship. The work of Constantin Brancusi, Henry Moore and Barbara Hepworth were influential in this, the latter being a particular source of inspiration for Riet Neevincz's biomorphic jewelry designs.

Throughout the 1950s and 1960s, with some leverage from the fine arts, jewelry in America and Europe developed a vocabulary to excite a wide variety of tastes. These ranged from cool Constructivist logic to energizing Abstract Expressionism, to the ethereal fantasies of

below
RIET NEEVINCZ
Brooch, 1964
Gold. W 4.5 cm

bottom
CHRIS STEENBERGEN
Brooch, 1952
Gold, silver. H 7.8 cm

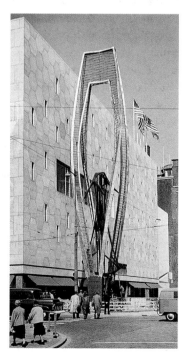

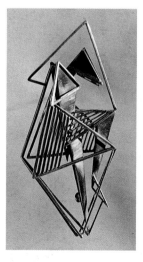

left
NAUM GABO
The Bijenkorf Construction outside Rotterdam's De Bijenkorf department store (designed by Marcel Breuer, 1956–57)

21

GIJS BAKKER
Large collar, 1967
Aluminium. W 40 cm

Surrealism. Yet, despite their many inventions, jewelers' interpretations of ornament were largely well mannered. There were some forays in American jewelry into subversion, principally by Sam Kramer, Ken Cory and Fred Woell, as well as in the bodyworks by Arline Fisch and Marjorie Schick. But in Europe, jewelers remained essentially makers of luxury objects from precious metals that functioned as adornment for the body, a situation that was to be challenged in 1967.

The work of two Dutch jewelers, Gijs Bakker and Emmy van Leersum, must dominate any account of jewelry of this period. Breaking with jewelry's past traditions, they waged an onslaught against elitism and orthodoxy, making a disruptive, uncompromising protest with large collars and bracelets in aluminium – a light, strong, malleable and cheap material. The choice was a deliberate social, aesthetic decision. This new democratic thinking, with its principles of minimal form devoid of embellishment, only became fully integrated when worn. Moreover, the body itself was considered part of the jewelry and not just its setting.

This assertive stance propelled Dutch jewelry on to the international stage. So strong and overwhelming was the work, and so convincing were its creators, that soon most of the jewelry fraternity in the Netherlands followed suit. There were many pale imitations, often indistinguishable from one another. However, there were notable practitioners whose work consolidated Bakker and van Leersum's approach. Nicolaas von Beck, Françoise van den Bosch, Bernhard Lameris, Hans Appenzeller, Frans van Nieuwenborg and Martijn Wegman are a few examples.

Marion Herbst, while acknowledging the best of these achievements, almost single-handedly opposed them. She celebrated the cause, but found the movement's all-pervasive interpretations clinical and repetitive. She felt that the intimidating hard-edged designs imposed too much on the wearer. Herbst's work was less formal and easier to wear: it had a colourful, mischievous, throwaway humour, characteristics which were later to endear her to some British jewelers.

Robert Smit's idiosyncratic approach also refused to conform to the van Leersum-Bakker approach. Using computerized drawings, Smit's jewelry in the late 1960s asserted a conceptual artistic mode realized in both acrylic and gold. Throughout most of the 1970s, he devoted his time to drawing, but returned to goldsmithing in the mid-1980s, creating an uproar with an exuberant return to the use of precious metals. This ran counter to current thinking in Dutch jewelry.

ITALY

During the Renaissance, Italian artists did not restrict themselves to a specific medium, but allowed their genius to spread beyond the confines of the canvas. Benvenuto Cellini, Andrea Mantegna and Leonardo da Vinci are examples of the great Italian masters who learned and practised the art of goldsmithing. Thus, Italy has enjoyed a tradition in which jewelry has been thought of as an art, providing stimulus not only for the eye, but also the mind.

As with other branches of Italian art, jewelry after the war caught the omnivorous eye and imagination of several painters and sculptors. For a time, this helped make Italy's contribution pre-eminent. Foremost among the Italian artists with quite different interpretations of jewelry were Afro and Lucio Fontana. Afro's enthusiasm for mural painting was successfully transferred to jewelry. With a primitive urgency, his work depicted animated hunting scenes drawn in a Palaeolithic style. Fontana's experiments in monochromatic painting in the 1940s later developed into his familiar slashed canvases. He applied this ferocious exuberance to jewelry to great effect, often brandishing a brutal and raw eroticism. In the 1960s his experiments with Minimalism in jewelry were extreme, echoing the curves and slashes of his painting.

Giorgio de Chirico, the Greek-born Surrealist, lived in Rome, where he began creating small bronze sculptures and jewelery in the 1960s, depicting the characters of his metaphysical world. While contemplating the haunting beauty of de Chirico's enigmas with their porticos and empty arcades, I am reminded of Salvador Dalì's ravishing exploits into jewelry in the 1950s, which were hailed with both enthusiasm and disbelief. The translation of his Surrealist images on to brooches – a pulsating heart, a jeweled eye, a floppy timepiece – caused a sensation when they were first shown. Pablo Picasso also made forays into jewelry with a few exceptional works of free drawing and mask-making in low relief.

Italy's influence in jewelry became increasingly important. Perhaps the most widely promoted were the brothers Giò and Arnaldo Pomodoro. Both ran large sculpture studios in Milan where ambitious projects were produced for shipment around the world. Alongside this they maintained their interest in jewelry which often mirrored the Abstract Expressionism dominating much of their thinking. Uninhibited in their use of form and scale, with strong sculptural textures cut deep into the metal, their jewelry demanded confident, emancipated women. The brothers' technique was influential and while there were many pale imitations of this new informality, positive influences can be seen in Andrew Grima's early work and Emanuel Raft's strong, sculptural jewelry, which he made in Sydney and London in the 1960s.

Bruno Martinazzi is both a sculptor and jeweler and his career, perhaps more than any other in Italy, conforms to the traditions of the Renaissance master. A deep vein of human confrontation runs through his work, whether analytical or sensual, in granite or gold. This interplay between psychic, physical and sexual forces orbits many of his ideas.

The work that placed Martinazzi before an international public exposed these sensitivities. Much of his jewelry depicted isolated parts of the human body, coining

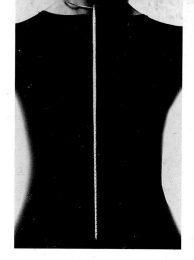

LUCIO FONTANA
Anti-Sofia, necklace, 1967
Gold. H 50 cm

below
BRUNO MARTINAZZI
Mouth Brooch, 1969
Gold. W 4.3 cm

bottom
Bruno Martinazzi mountaineering in Aosta,
Italy, 1948

top
POL BURY
Bracelet, 1968
Gold with moving spheres. Plaque 5 x 5 cm

above
POL BURY
Necklace-brooch, 1968
Gold with moving filaments. H 17 cm

them as symbols, some of which warned of society's ills: Mouth as symbolic of greed, Fist as the focus of forces, Lips representing affection, Buttocks charged with eroticism, Hands and Fingers as instruments of human invention and the terminals of intelligence, and Eyes as the soul's manifested beauty and our visual perception of the world. These subjects, portrayed in 'classical' forms, were also the images for large-scale stone carvings for land and cityscapes. But their subversive character worked best as jewelry, where the ideas came full circle, returning to their source – the human body.

One can only hazard a guess at how far this boost from the fine arts energized and influenced other jewelers' work. The Pomodoro brothers, Calder, Dalì and Picasso were promoted internationally, but most other jewelers received infrequent international exposure.

In Rome, the entrepreneur and jewelry manufacturer Mario Masenza was an early patron of art jewelry in the 1950s. He commissioned artists to produce designs that were executed in his workshops and then offered for sale in his shops. With a degree of pragmatism, the Pomodoro brothers extended Masenza's thinking in the 1960s by encouraging their brother-in-law, Gian Carlo Montebello, in his initiative to promote jewelry by fine artists. In 1967 he established GEM Montebello in Milan, equipped with workshops and craftsmen to translate the artists' designs into limited editions, an enterprise that captured a new and expanding market. His stable of artists included Pol Bury, César, Pietro Consagra, Lucio del Pezzo, Amalia del Ponte, Lucio Fontana, Niki de Saint-Phalle, Man Ray, Hans Richter, Richard Smith, Jesús-Rafael Soto, Ettore Sottsass, Joe Tilson and, of course, the Pomodoro brothers. Not all these famous artists' ideas translated well into jewelry, but they helped to stimulate its spirit. As a postscript, Montebello explained to me that when Alexander Calder was asked to contribute designs for these editions, he declined, stating that he made his jewelry for fun and not on demand.

So far, we have only looked at jewelry in Italy from painters and sculptors. Yet there were men (with a noticeable absence of women) who devoted their creative energies to goldsmithing – traditionally a largely male occupation. There is no creative centre comparable with Pforzheim for jewelry in Italy, but there is a coterie of talent surrounding Padua, where Mario Pinton was born and where he lives today.

During the aftermath of the war, when Pinton set up his studio, designers were looking forwards rather than backwards for inspiration. Many scrutinized developments in science and technology, as well as the abstraction that was informing much of the contemporary fine arts. Yet Pinton opted for a reversal of this international trend and looked afresh at antiquity. During the 1950s, he produced mainly figurative work, with finely drawn low reliefs of human and animal forms based on his interpretation of Egyptian and Etruscan imagery. There were other Italian artists

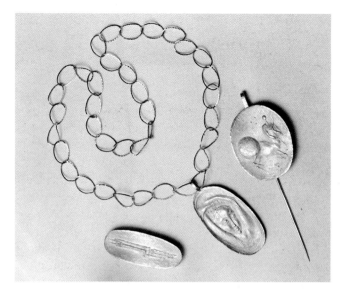

MARIO PINTON
Brooch, pendant and hat pin, 1959–60
Gold. H 9 cm, 8 cm and 7 cm

whose work also strove to readdress the past, among them the sculptor Marino Marini, with whom Pinton had once worked. Marini's bronze horsemen echo Etruscan and ancient Chinese art.

Anton Frühauf, like Pinton, looked to the past and explored Greek mythology, dissecting pictorial elements and reconstructing them with stylized reliefs almost to the point of total abstraction. He eventually moved away from figuration altogether, towards an Abstract Expressionist style. In the 1970s, he compressed dense organic structures into jewelry; these pieces, despite their small scale, expressed massive energy.

Francesco Pavan was a former student of Mario Pinton. At the chance suggestion of his father's bookseller, Pavan entered art school in Padua to study goldsmithing at the age of twelve, graduating at eighteen. To earn his living, he became an assistant in Pinton's studio, but was smitten with modern sculpture, particularly the rhythmic, kinetic work of Jesús-Rafael Soto and the radical expressions of Lucio Fontana. He met Fontana one Sunday afternoon 'simply by picking up the 'phone'. A visit was arranged, and Pavan, who had brought along some friends for moral support, was greeted by the painter with 'great warmth and openness . . . Fontana's large white studio was full of his slashed canvases . . . I remember my heart thumping away with the sheer excitement of the place, it was inspirational.'

Pavan's passion for modern art in the 1960s became a strong influence on his own work; caught up by its liberating spirit, his designs developed a cool, simplifying ethos, a puritanical aesthetic more in line with Dutch or Scandinavian sensitivities.

European studio jewelers in the 1950s and 1960s attempted to rescue their craft from the clichés of traditional design. With the notable exception of Bakker and van Leersum, jewelers projected an inventive spirit but kept largely within the parameters of goldsmithing techniques and jewelry's conventional scale. But things were soon to change.

CHAPTER III
EUROPEAN CROSS CURRENTS, 1970–1980

In a blizzard of egos, graduates emerged from art schools in the 1970s to scale the boundaries set by the previous generation. New materials and methods were found, declaring jewelry's independence from wealth, status and fashion. A growing international awareness encouraged radical experiments, with some jewelers testing the limits of function, while others decamped, expressing interest in other fields.

In the Netherlands, van Leersum and Bakker continued to expand the debate concerning jewelry's role in society with work of Minimalist, industrial refinement. Later, Bakker broadened his thinking through ironic photographic interpretations of status jewelry, sports icons and overblown, voluptuous flowers. Others in Holland also explored industrial methods and produced editions using actual industrial components in their jewelry. Hans Appenzeller and Lous Martin were amongst the first to use textiles, rubber and aluminium. They opened the Gallery Sieraad to promote their own work and others like it. Marion Herbst's Shower Tube bracelet of 1971, the Zip necklaces of 1972 by Martijn Wegman and Frans van Nieuwenborg and Paul Derrez's 1976 Spiral Pins (all shown on this page) were forerunners in Holland of this democratic approach. There were others, including Maria Hees and Marga Staartjes, who were later to use cheap industrial products, such as plastic brushes and pan-scourers in their stylish and inventive jewelry. This close relationship to industry led several studio jewelers in Holland – Gijs Bakker, Herman Hermsen, Bruno Ninaber van Eyben and Hans Appenzeller – to expand their interests in product design.

In Britain, the crafts and industry remained largely incompatible, although there were exceptions. In 1970, at the time of Wendy Ramshaw's first solo show, studio jewelry was still largely made by hand. William Morris's loathing of the machine clung with such persistence to craft practices that when Ramshaw first switched on an electric lathe to turn metal, eyebrows were raised in some circles.

Undeterred, she set out tenaciously to build a career as an artist in jewelry. This early period in her career was exciting, with work that strove to achieve a balance between the perfection produced by a machine and the individual, unique characteristics wrought by hand. The seeds for her popular success were her inventive adaptation of an ancient practice, where clusters of rings are worn on separate fingers or grouped together on one. Ramshaw refined the idea, running through a whole range of coloured, enamelled variations with strong linear imagery. The permutations of her ring-set arrangements are endless and engage the wearer in a degree of choice. Pragmatically solving the problem of display, she evolved the idea of display mounts, which developed into the now recognized enamelled trophies that carry her work. Claiming the status of artist for the jeweler, her relentless attempts at rapprochement with the fine arts brought further accolades in the 1980s with a series of jewels inspired by Picasso's later portraits of women.

In Germany, in 1971, Nuremberg marked the 500th anniversary of the birth of Albrecht Dürer. As he and his father had been goldsmiths, one of the celebrations was

WENDY RAMSHAW
Pendant with Sunderland bridge background, 1970
Silver, pale amethysts. H 8 cm

(from left to right)
HERBST, VAN NIEUWENBORG, WEGMAN, DERREZ
'Industrial' pieces in chrome-plated copper, steel and silver, 1971–76

a major international jewelry exhibition. Many of the great names in contemporary goldsmithing took part, including some young unknowns: Claus Bury, Ulrike Bahrs, Onno Boekhoudt, Jens-Rudiger Lorenzen, Wendy Ramshaw, Gerd Rothmann and Hubertus von Skal. All, with the exception of Ramshaw (who was self-taught), were fresh-faced goldsmithing graduates from Germany's prestigious academies.

The catalogue to this exhibition captures the changing attitudes in jewelry. There was an air of freedom about the work of these young jewelers, as formality gave way to liberating influences from technology and the fine arts.

Bury and Rothmann threw down the gauntlet. They challenged the traditions of goldsmithing with brilliantly coloured Pop art imagery. Dispensing with precious materials, they turned uncompromisingly to acrylic sheet. In an exhibition of goldsmithing of this calibre, it was unprecedented. Bury and Rothmann, who were joined later by the Austrian Fritz Maierhofer, were neither the first nor the last jewelers to use acrylic in their work, though they were undoubtedly the most impressive. All three later augmented gold into their work with hard-edged graphic imagery, diagrams and symbols.

Even by German standards, Bury was a brilliant goldsmith with breathtaking technique. He is also a fine draughtsman and colourist – skills that he employed to expand the conceptual parameters of jewelry. Using gold, acrylic and metal patination, his subliminal work in the 1970s had a cool, mechanized quality. This often included visual interpretations of architectural perspective. In the previous chapter I mentioned Bury's influence in America. His ideas were also acutely felt in Europe, particularly in Britain. Young goldsmiths Ros Conway, Roger Morris, Gunilla Treen and Pierre Degen admired his approach. But by the end of the decade, Bury had exhausted his interest in jewelry and began to concentrate solely on sculpture.

As demonstrated in the Dürer exhibition, Onno Boekhoudt and Jens-Rudiger Lorenzen still retained a foothold in goldsmithing traditions through their continued use of precious metals. However, their Modernist compositions moved jewelry forward. Boekhoudt's smooth, abstract shapes hinted at Minimalism, reflecting his Dutch background. But the influence of Rienhold Reiling, with whom he studied at Pforzheim, was also present. Lorenzen had already arrived at a self-assured style that would be the hallmark of his work through the next decade. He aggressively shattered all the 'prettiness' that can be associated with jewelry by his dramatic piercing and splitting of metal. This approach perhaps owed something to Fontana.

Hubertus von Skal was 29 years old at this time. Born in Czechoslovakia, he went to Germany in the 1960s and settled there. Like Martinazzi's and Jünger's work, von Skal works within the confines of goldsmithing. Here, function and materials are orthodox, yet the work places ideas higher than the value of the materials used. Conceptually, von Skal's jewelry is a synthesis of his personal obsessions. He explores

JENS-RUDIGER LORENZEN
Brooch, 1968
Polished and grey oxidized silver, red varnish.
H 7.5 cm

CLAUS BURY
Brooch, 1972
Gold, acrylic. H 11.5 cm
Schmuckmuseum, Pforzheim

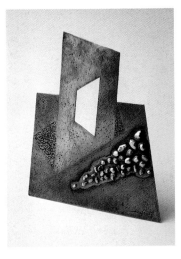

HUBERTUS VON SKAL
Miniature, 1968
Silver. H 10 cm

symbolism and metaphor and makes eclectic references with authority and an astonishing continuity that spans more than thirty years. There is also a Surrealist element in some of his work.

Subconscious, ethereal and symbolic expression are also to be found in the work of Ulrike Bahrs, who, like von Skal, lives in Munich. Using a wide range of materials (onyx, opal, ebony, lapis lazuli and jade), which already suggests an ancient and historic symbolism, she instills an extra and personal allegory into her rich figurative collages.

Bahrs's love of materials and figuration is shared by the English jeweler, Charlotte de Syllas, who studied under Gerda Flöckinger. According to de Syllas, Flöckinger was a hard taskmaster who made her look at things for herself! This 'learning to look' is not restricted to the inanimate, but includes a close study of people. Most, if not all, of de Syllas's jewelry is made to commission; the personality of the wearer becomes an integral part of the character of the piece. For some artists, this aspect of commissioning has become something of a cliché, but for de Syllas it is crucial. When commissioned by an institution, she looks at the character and persona of the building. For an important Victoria and Albert Museum commission, for example, she designed a pearl and coral choker, very much with an old Victorian lady in mind. I knew of her reputation for acquiring painstaking skills, especially those concerned with carving, and I asked her whether this was an obsession or devotion to her craft. 'Definitely a passion,' she said. The gestation period for her commissions can be lengthy and in her thirty-year career she has made fewer than forty pieces.

Reinforcing the seriousness and status of craft practices in Europe, the 1970s will be remembered as a forward-looking decade, with new galleries and institutions being formed. We will look at these developments on the Continent later. In Britain, the Crafts Advisory Committee (now The Crafts Council) was formed in 1971. In the same year, the Electrum Gallery opened in London. It was an obsession of mine. Its planning took a year, with its first four formative years under my artistic direction. My business partner, Barbara Cartlidge, and I strove to build a forum for jewelry to present its avant-garde. The gallery was to take not an insular but a global perspective when preparing its exhibitions. This policy energized British jewelry, and, as we will discover, led to an exchange of influences between countries.

Central to Electrum's concerns at that time was an ideology shared by its contributors, which attempted to attack the issues we felt were irksome: that jewelry was equated with wealth; that chainstore jewelry stylistically emulated more expensive 'upper class' versions; that expensive jewelry was bought predominantly by men for women, to display the man's wealth and the woman as his possession. Moreover, most jewelry was redundant of ideas or the power to challenge. We decided, therefore, that there would be no restrictions in terms of materials. We would encourage innovation and celebrate jewelry for both sexes.

Not all activity promoting jewelry was focused in London. In Philadelphia, Helen Drutt established an outlet for American crafts which later also became a regular yet rare exhibition venue on the East Coast for American and European goldsmiths. Back in the UK, in Bristol, Sarah Osborn became the jewelry co-ordinator at Bristol's Arnolfini gallery, where she organized several provocative exhibitions and events. Arnolfini in fact had shown studio jewelry since the gallery's inception in 1961 (although they no longer do so).

Textiles have been used extensively for many centuries for spectacular ornament for either sex, whether as part of dress, ruffs and collars, or independently as jewelry. David Poston's use of fibre in the early 1970s, however, brought out other qualities in textiles that had hardly been recognized. He began to re-examine the social dimensions of jewelry with its emphasis on wealth and status. This led to tactile experiments intended to benefit the wearer, not the spectator. Abandoning most precious metals – rejecting gold emphatically because of South African exploitation of black labour in mining – he began working in string, hemp and cotton and in bone and leather. The results were not just warm and sensual, but had an elegance and frugal modesty born out of the maker's commitment.

Poston's explorations highlight the issue that the materials with which an object is made influence our evaluation of it. This is certainly true of jewelry where the intrinsic value of the material can get in the way of our aesthetic perception. As Dr Johnson said, 'You would not value the finest head if carved upon a carrot.' Yet what, I wonder, would the great man have made of Gijs Bakker's early work or others in this survey, who rate ideas and their realization above the cost of materials used? Perhaps there are double standards at work here, for this carrot-carving argument hardly applies to the fine arts, where the intrinsic value of materials is of little consequence.

This issue led to protracted arguments in the 1970s, particularly in Holland and Britain. But the democratic approach did not receive universal support. In Germany and Austria, for example, the spirited investigations of Bury, Maierhofer and Rothmann into non-precious materials were ruled more by aesthetic than ideological considerations. They had pushed acrylics to the limit, but that done, the goldsmiths returned to their precious materials as ducks to water.

In Italy, radical democratic arguments surrounding jewelry hardly arose. Its avant-garde jeered at design conventions chiefly through the furniture and ceramics of the Memphis group, egged on by Ettore Sottsass. In comparison with the rest of Europe, Italian goldsmiths often appear more retrospective. Certainly there is a consistency in the spirit of innovation that links Italy's past with its present. Frühauf, Pavan, Pinton, Martinazzi and the Pomodoro brothers contributed to international jewelry throughout this period. But the man who successfully reinvented Italy's long traditions in goldsmithing at this time was Giampaolo Babetto.

GIAMPAOLO BABETTO
Necklace, 1968
Gold. H 32.5 cm

The Boe Group, Amsterdam, 1974
(from left to right) Onno Boekhoudt, Karel
Niehorster, Françoise van den Bosch, Marion
Herbst, Berend Peters

Assimilating classical proportions with modernity, Babetto's gold jewelry has a strong sculptural presence. Stripped of embellishments, its character relies on proportion and generosity of scale. There is a serene potency about this authoritative work, which, despite its size, is reminiscent of Minimalist sculpture. Notwithstanding these references, Babetto's jewelry is eminently wearable. The affinity between sculpture and goldsmithing was also explored by Elisabeth Holder and Daniel Kruger. Holder's interpretation of Modernism brought hard-edged sculptural solutions to rings and necklaces with a designer's restraint. Kruger's approach was more conceptual, often relying on the shock value of unlikely materials, such as in his leather and silk pouches filled with stones.

During the 1970s, the diminishing of the earth's resources and the protection of its wildlife lacked the high profile it has today. Ivory, for example, was widely used in the jewelry trade and by designers such as David Poston and Caroline Broadhead. Eventually this was to change as people became aware of the threatening situation. Broadhead's brief flirtation with ivory was lighthearted and tinged with Pop art imagery – carved 'knots' and 'dribbles' and the like. Impressed by David Poston's experiments, she started to use fibre in gloriously celebratory colours, which formed a series of jewelry editions. (The Dutch government's purchasing policy had long enabled jewelers to make jewelry more available to a wider audience.) Inspired by this, Broadhead joined Susanna Heron, Nuala Jamieson and Julia Manheim in organizing 'Fourways' (1977–79), a touring exhibition of jewelry editions. This pragmatism enabled the four British jewelers to show their work more widely, which helped support experimental designs.

Diversifying from natural fibre, Broadhead started to construct jewelry with tufted nylon monofilaments. In pushing the material to its limits, she found herself encroaching on the territory of clothing. She began to basket-weave the material into highly flexible collars and bracelets which, when pulled up over the arm or head became meshed protective structures, like veils or sleeves. This developed into ambiguous experiments with clothing that emphasized the process and the repetitive movements made in dressing. It gradually brought her work to performance art where issues surrounding gender and stereotypes were addressed.

Susanna Heron's authority in the use of colour revealed the influence of her father, Patrick Heron. She also showed an acute sense of proportion; her silver and resin jewelry always looked comfortable with itself and with the wearer, the relation of jewelry to the body being of great importance to her.

In the late 1970s, she and her former husband, the artist David Ward, travelled extensively in the USA for a year. Experimenting with prototypes for bracelets and necklaces, new jewelry was later realized with acrylic and sprayed paint as a vehicle for translucency, light and colour. Exploring the tenuous and sometimes ambiguous relationship between clothing and jewelry, Heron made a collection of 'ruff' or 'cape' forms from painted papier-mâché, cotton or nylon. For some of these she coined the term 'wearables'. These pieces, which hovered on the brink of function, were her last experiments with jewelry forms. She now makes sculpture.

By the late 1970s, British work, formerly seen as inferior to that of the Continent, moved into position and began to attract international attention. In comparison with Holland, British jewelry was far less stylistically consistent, motivated by individual dissent rather than any movement or group.

In 1976, Paul Derrez opened Galerie Ra in Amsterdam, soon to become the flagship of international jewelry's avant-garde. He became a frequent visitor to English studios and brought the 'Fourways' exhibition to the Netherlands. The show burst upon an unexpectant public, some of which had serious reservations about the British approach, which was seen as lighthearted. Nonetheless, influences could soon be detected in new Dutch jewelry, particularly in work from the textile fraternity. Marion Herbst was among the first to appreciate this British individuality. She was drawn particularly to the work of Poston and Broadhead, who both used colourful fibre in their work. Later, Herbst was to produce a series of embroidered brooches which parodied military decorations.

Mecky van den Brink and Lam de Wolf were not trained as jewelers, but they adopted the craft, with their work reflecting their studies in textiles. Fibre adapted well to their ideas, particularly the enigmatic work by de Wolf, which trod the boundaries between ornament, performance and installation. Similar explorations were also partly dealt with later by Joke Brakman and Claudie Berbee, developing inventive new ways of dress fastenings that parodied ornament.

David Watkins, Professor of Jewellery and Metalwork at the Royal College of Art, has had little formal training in goldsmithing, but studied sculpture. In the 1970s he was an unrelenting Modernist, a disciplinarian of the purest design aesthetic, producing stylish jewelry collections from lathe-turned, dyed acrylic. His work transformed the industrial material and introduced to British jewelry a clarity and authority to rival the Dutch and German schools. Later he reverted to metal and introduced a collection of interlocking steel body and neck pieces, in blue steel and gold, that echoed the sparseness of architectural drawings. In the early 1980s, colour flooded his linear works, among which were his multiple necklaces made from neoprene-coated steel in a strong Postmodernist style. Eric Spiller was also an early exponent of a reductivist style in British jewelry in the 1970s. His consistent analytical approach might be regarded as structural Minimalism, with ideas kept simple but extremely effective.

Julia Manheim had previously been known for her sensuously carved jewelry. In the early 1980s, she started to work with acrylics, leading to explorations with larger

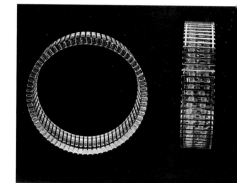

ERIC SPILLER
Bracelet, 1972
Rhodium-plated brass, glass ball bearings.
Dia 7.6 cm

DAVID WATKINS
Hinged interlocking body piece, 1976
Steel. H 50 cm

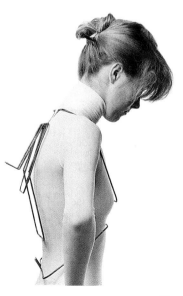

body pieces constructed from plastic-coated wire. Like Broadhead and Heron, she began to consider jewelry's relationship with dress, but with quite different results – brightly painted tabards and body pieces with an air of optimistic ambiguity about them. She also later abandoned her interest in jewelry to become a sculptor.

Pierre Degen continued this British emphasis on diversity and innovation. With Claus Bury as an early influence, Degen freely applied his imagination in the 1970s with little regard for traditions or boundaries. Fastening mechanisms became an integral aesthetic consideration in his work. 'Hooking' brooches and 'tension' bracelets had taut thin lines of thread or steel, casting shadows across the body. Bandages of coarse, graphitic linen wrapped the wrists tightly, binding in place found objects. In the early 1980s, he let rip with bold and controversial experiments which outraged many. Those who searched frantically for a meaning were looking in the wrong direction: Degen's performance-based work was never intended as commercial ornament, but showed his fascination with everyday objects and materials that usually go unobserved. His constructions were on a grand scale but always composed with meticulous attention. Such vision provided stimulus for more orthodox, commercial jewelers and his work has been misinterpreted by artists who have extracted his visual vocabulary from its context for their own use, often with unsuccessful and pretentious results.

Thus the changing condition of jewelry throughout the 1980s brought us to conceptual work where the communication of ideas stood before aesthetics. Otto Künzli, the Swiss-born goldsmith, became the leading exponent of jewelry of this genre, sceptically skirting around conventional jewelry with its emphasis on status. He also questioned what he considered to be the more pretentious 'studio' jewelry of his contemporaries by keeping most of his own work within the notional parameters of function. His investigations were often cynical, investing ideas and materials with irony, wryly examining symbols and icons, particularly of America's diverse culture. This included a body of work which dented the image of the great Disney ambassador, Mickey Mouse.

One of Künzli's most poignant works was made as early as 1980. Gold Makes Blind consists of a black rubber bangle with an obvious single lump, which we are told encases a gold ball. The parallels between this masking of the gold and the bullion, stored deep underground, protecting the balance of the world's economy, symbolizes the arbitrary properties with which we invest this material.

The 1980s witnessed the most radical spirit in jewelry's history. The forms that jewelry could take were expanded and its practical limits tested. New work arose which drew further on jewelry's relationship to the body and to clothing. This led some jewelers to performance-based work and photographic jewelry events, where control over aspects of wearing jewelry are fixed in a single image.

left
BARBARA MORGAN
Photograph of Martha Graham
in Letter to the World (Kick), 1940

below
ED WIENER
The Dancer, brooch, 1948
Silver. H 6.7 cm
Musée des Arts Décoratifs, Montreal

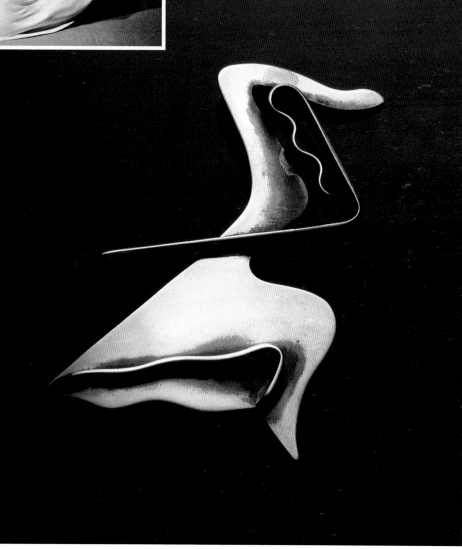

SAM KRAMER
Roc Pendant, 1957
Sterling silver, gold, ivory, horn, coral,
taxidermy eye, tourmaline, garnet. H 12 cm
American Crafts Museum, New York

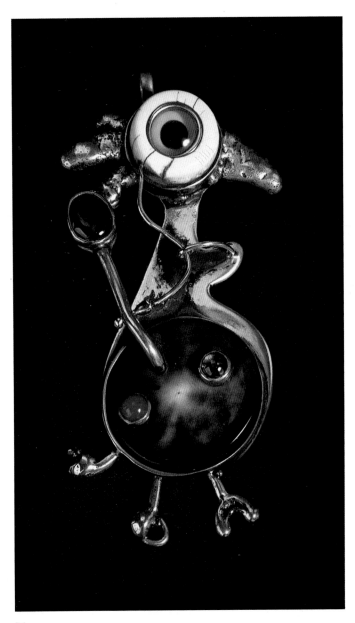

above
ART SMITH
Bracelet, c. 1948
Copper, brass. L 10.4 cm
Musée des Arts Décoratifs, Montreal

right
ALEXANDER CALDER
Brooch, c. 1955
Silver. L 13.3 cm

right (inset)
ALEXANDER CALDER
Shirt studs, c. 1936–39
Brass. Dia 3.1 cm
Museum of Fine Arts, Boston

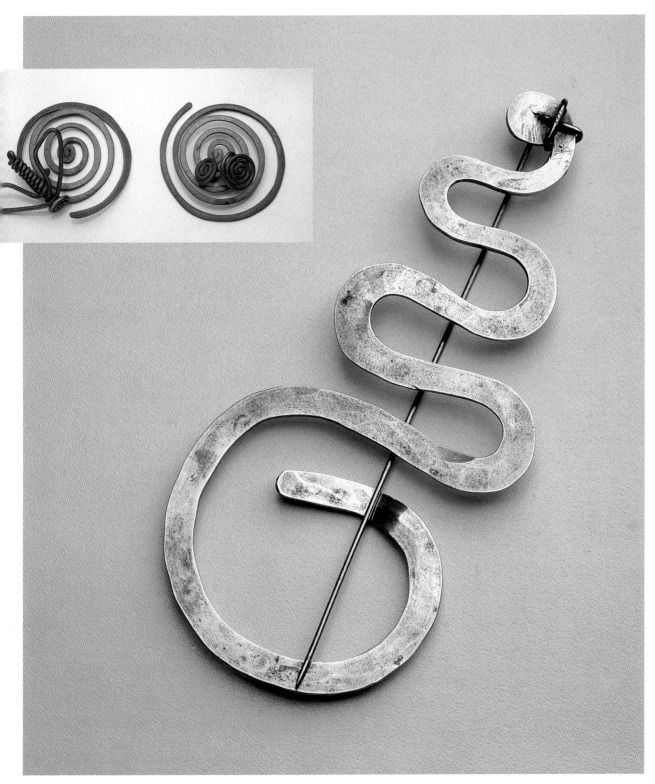

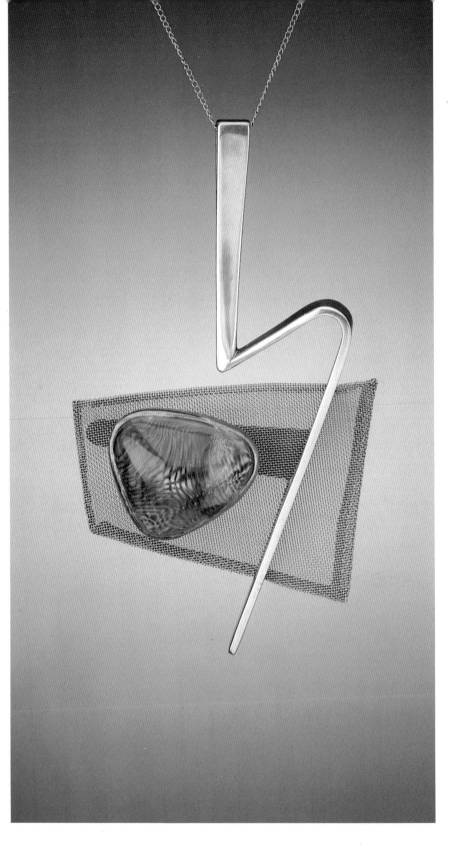

above
MARGARET DE PATTA
Brooch, *c.* 1947–50
Sterling silver, coral, malachite. W 9 cm
American Crafts Museum, New York

right
MARGARET DE PATTA
Pendant, 1951
Sterling silver screen, stainless steel, crystal.
H 6.5 cm
Oakland Museum of California

MERRY RENK
Building, brooch, 1948
Silver, enamel. H 4.1 cm
Musée des Arts Décoratifs, Montreal

EARL PARDON
Pendant with collar, c. 1955
Silver, rosewood. H 22.9 cm
Musée des Arts Décoratifs, Montreal

HARRY BERTOIA
Brooch, 1942
Silver. H 9.1 cm
Musée des Arts Décoratifs, Montreal

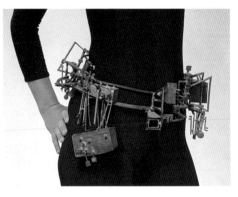

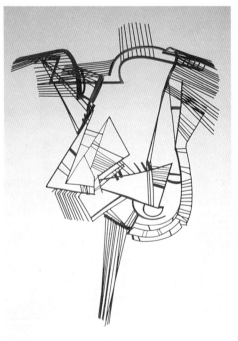

above and right
MARJORIE SCHICK
Pectoral body piece, 1968–69
Brass, bronze. H 64 cm

BARRY S. MERRITT
Deco Queen, 1973
Fibreglass, lacquer, leather, silver, brass, bronze,
moonstone, amethyst, ruby crystal. H 40 cm

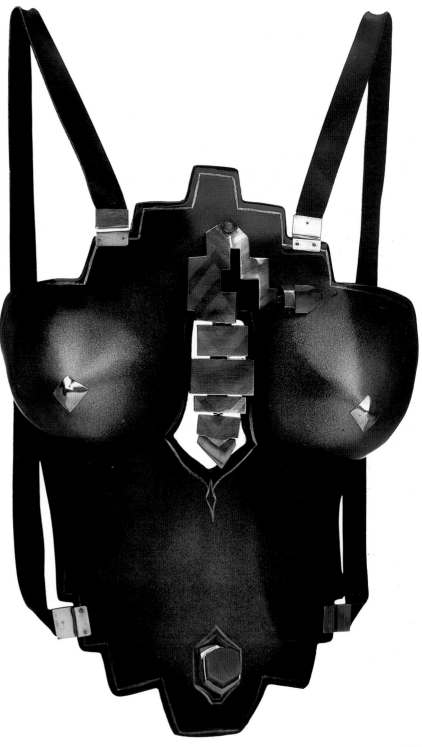

right
FRED WOELL
Come Alive, You're in the Pepsi Generation,
brooch, 1966
Silver, copper, brass. H 10 cm

below
FRED WOELL
November 22, 1963, 12.30 pm, brooch
mounted in frame, 1967
Copper, silver, brass, gold leaf, photo, wood.
H 16 cm
National Museum of American Art,
Smithsonian Institution, Washington

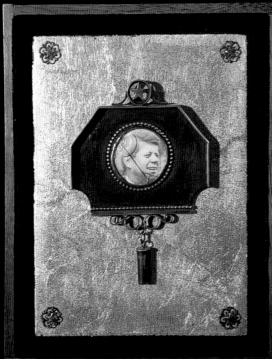

left
ROBERT EBENDORF
Man and His Pet Bee, brooch, 1971
Copper, carnelian beads. H 17 cm

below
ROBERT EBENDORF
Mother and Child, brooch, 1971
Copper, sterling silver, paper, plexiglass.
Dia 12 cm

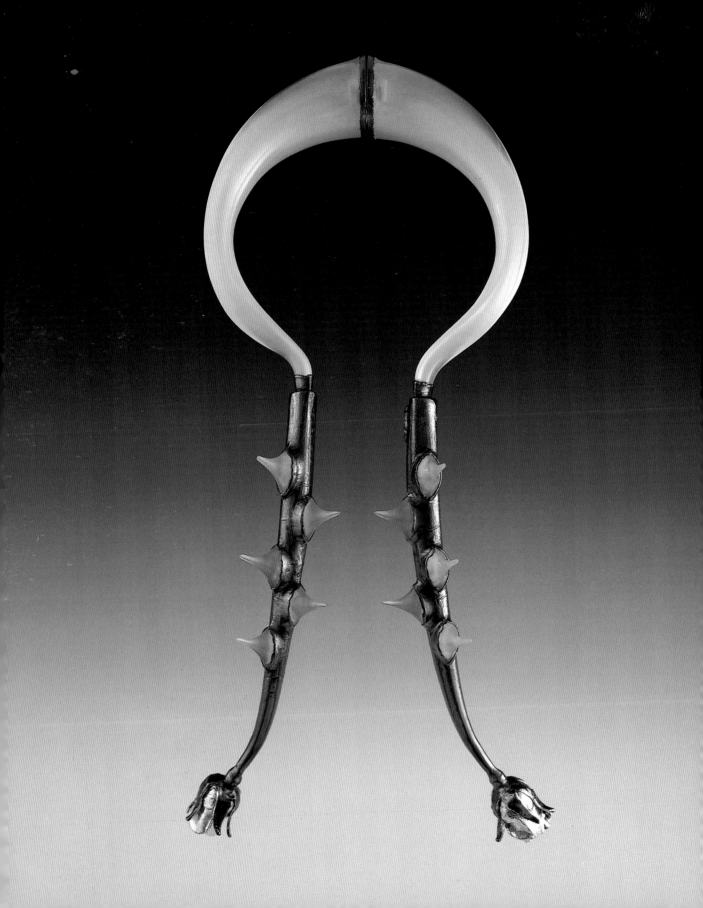

left
STANLEY LECHTZIN
Rose Torque, 1973
Silver, polyester resin. H 44.5 cm

right
JOHN PAUL MILLER
Armoured Polyp, 1969
Gold and enamel with granulation and textile
collar. H 7.5 cm
American Crafts Museum, New York

below right
MARGRET CRAVER
Eclosion Brooch, 1964
Gold *en résille*. W 6.5 cm
Minneapolis Museum of Art

left
STANLEY LECHTZIN
Brooch, 1970
Silver gilt, agate. W 23 cm
Worshipful Company of Goldsmiths,
London

right
ALBERT PALEY
Necklace, 1973
Forged and fabricated sterling silver with
gold inlay, gold, copper, glass opal, Delrin.
H 53 cm

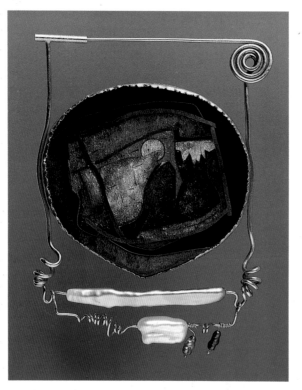

left
WILLIAM HARPER
Grey Mystery, brooch, 1978
Gold, silver, cloisonné enamel on copper.
H 9.7 cm

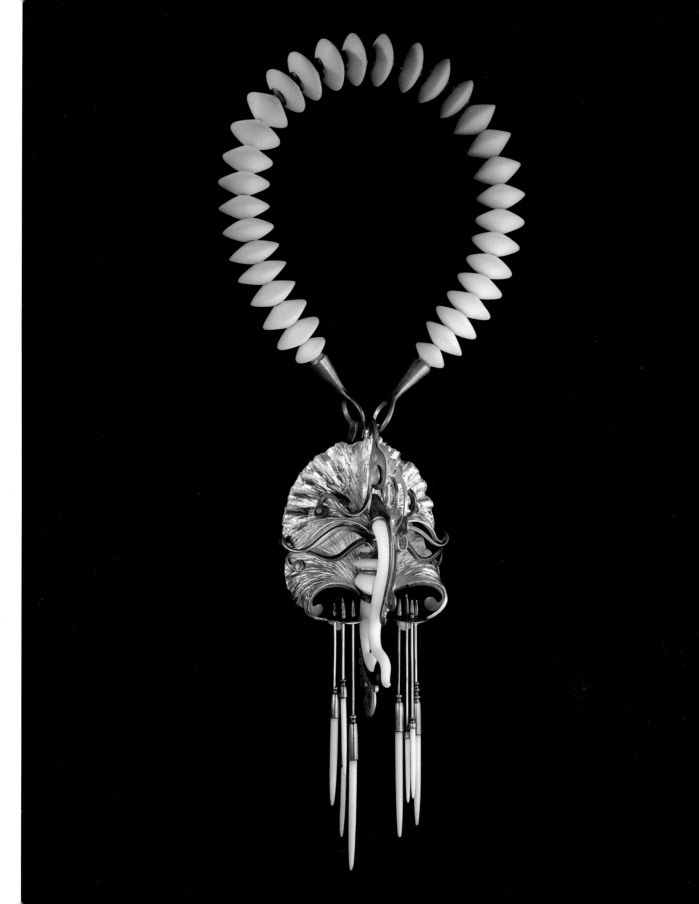

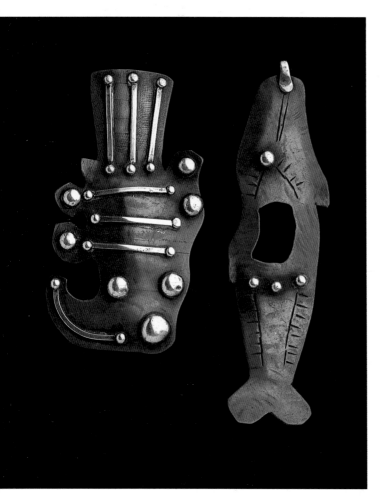

left
ALAN DAVIE
Bird and Fish, brooches, 1950
Copper, silver. H 7.5 cm and 9.5 cm

below
WILLIAM SCOTT
Pendant and chain, 1961
Gold. H of pendant, 7.6 cm
Victoria and Albert Museum, London

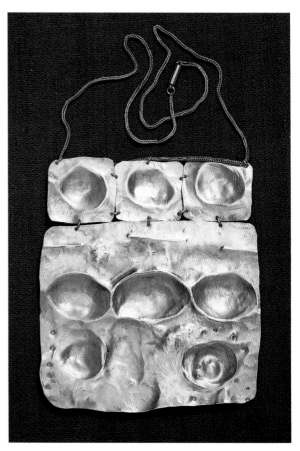

above
ROBERT ADAMS
Brooch, 1961
Silver gilt. H 9 cm
Worshipful Company
of Goldsmiths, London

above
ELIZABETH FRINK
Pendant worn on a leather thong, 1961
Bronze. H 12.7 cm
Victoria and Albert Museum, London

left
TERRY FROST
Necklace, 1960
Silver. L 33 cm
Victoria and Albert Museum, London

47

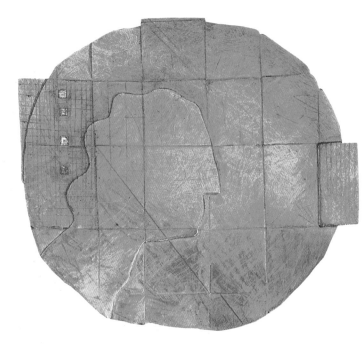

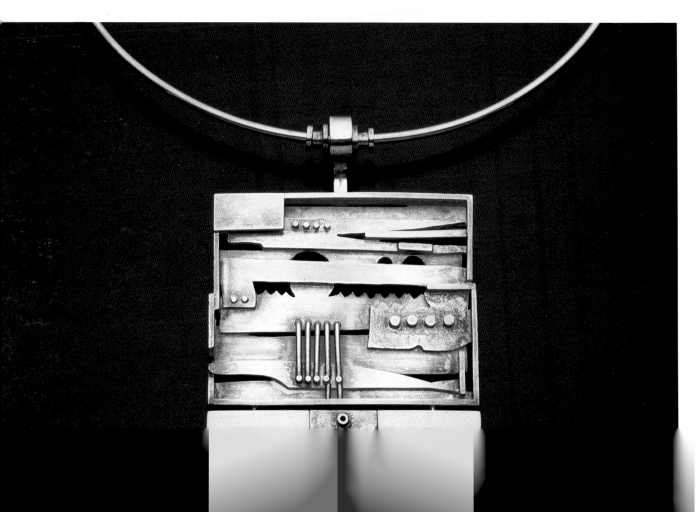

below
GERDA FLÖCKINGER
Neckband, 1968
Silver, gold, cabochon, tourmalines, aquamarine,
smokey quartz, garnets, pearls. Dia 12 cm

above
HELGA ZAHN
Neckpiece with collar, 1973
Silver, amber, nylon monofilament. L 38 cm
Crafts Council, London

right
HELGA ZAHN
Pendant with collar, 1965
Silver set with arrowhead and pebble. H 31 cm
Worshipful Company of Goldsmiths, London

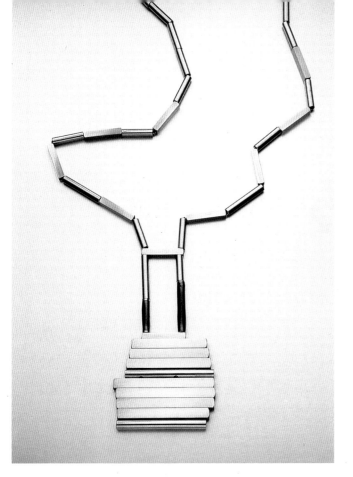

left
NAUM SLUTZKY
Pendant, *c.* 1961
Silver bands, blue enamel. W 5 cm
Worshipful Company of Goldsmiths, London

below left
HERMANN JÜNGER
Brooch, *c.* 1968
Silver, enamel. H 7.3 cm
Schmuckmuseum, Pforzheim

below
HERMANN JÜNGER
Brooch, 1967
Gold, enamel. H 4.6 cm
Schmuckmuseum, Pforzheim

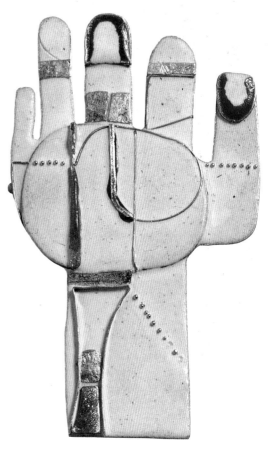

above
FRANÇOISE VAN DEN BOSCH
Bracelet, 1970
Aluminium. Dia 10 cm
Stedelijk Museum, Amsterdam

left
EMMY VAN LEERSUM
Fold bracelets, 1969
Aluminium. H 7 cm
Stedelijk Museum, Amsterdam

MARION HERBST
Necklace, 1969
Silver, acrylic. H 18 cm
Museum Het Kruithuis, 's Hertogenbosch

below
ROBERT SMIT
Brooch and ring, 1970
Acrylic and gold. 7 x 7 cm and 4 x 4 cm

left
LUCIO FONTANA
Ellisse, bracelets, 1967
Left, silver oval with holes, white-lacquered
Right, silver oval with slash cut, turquoise-lacquered. H 15.6 cm

left, centre
SALVADOR DALÌ
The Eye of Time, watch and brooch, c. 1949
Platinum, diamonds, ruby, blue enamel. W 6.4 cm
Minami Jewellery Museum, Kamakura, Japan

left, bottom
PABLO PICASSO
Bull's Head, brooch, c. 1950
Gold. H 5 cm

below
GIORGIO DE CHIRICO
Pendant, 1964
Silver. H 7 cm

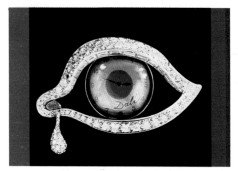

below
ARNALDO POMODORO
Brooch, 1958
Gold. W 8.5 cm

right
ARNALDO POMODORO
Pendant, 1966
Gold, white gold. L 17.5 cm
Schmuckmuseum, Pforzheim

bottom
BRUNO MARTINAZZI
Goldfinger, bracelet, 1973
White and yellow gold. H 8.7 cm
Schmuckmuseum, Pforzheim

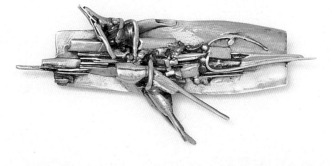

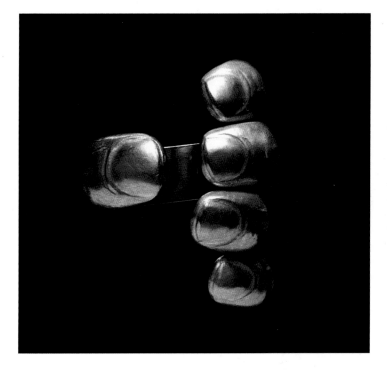

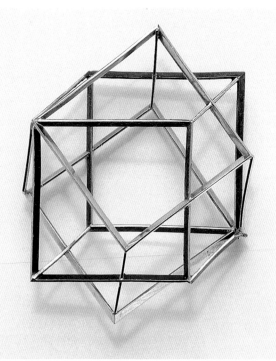

FRANCESCO PAVAN
Brooch, 1972
White gold. W 7.6 cm

ANTON FRÜHAUF
Pendant, 1970
Gold. H 7.2 cm

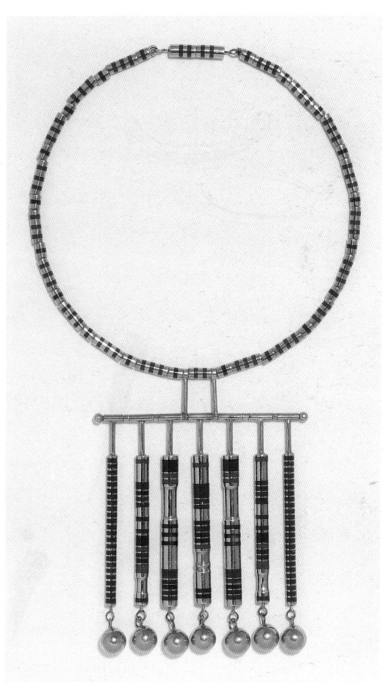

above
WENDY RAMSHAW
Set of five rings, 1970
Gold, enamel. H 5 cm

right
WENDY RAMSHAW
Necklace and pendant, 1971
Gold, enamel. H of pendant 16.5 cm
Victoria and Albert Museum, London

CLAUS BURY
Brooch, 1969
Acrylic. H 7.5 cm
Deutsches Goldschmiedehaus, Hanau

below
CLAUS BURY
Brooch, 1973
Gold. H 6.3 cm
Schmuckmuseum, Pforzheim

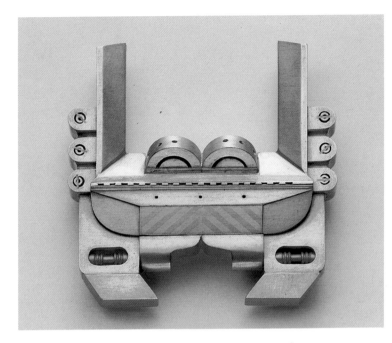

below left
GERD ROTHMANN
Brooches, 1970
Steel, acrylic. H 5.5 cm

below
ONNO BOEKHOUDT
Jewelry Object, 1970
Silver, stainless steel. H 9 cm

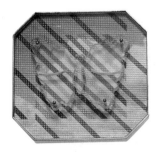

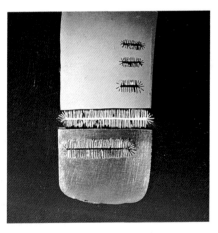

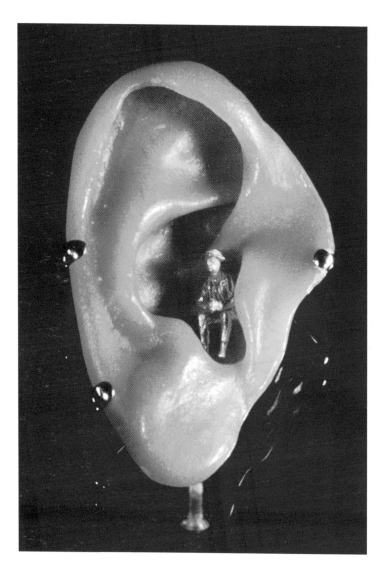

right
CHARLOTTE DE SYLLAS
Two views of Annie's Necklace, 1974
Black jade, opal, quartz. H 24 cm

bottom right, from left to right
CHARLOTTE DE SYLLAS
Head Ring (boxed in hands), 1968
Gold, carved agate. H 7 cm

far right
ULRIKE BAHRS
Hommage à la jeune femme, brooch, 1976
(Homage to the Young Woman)
Gold, silver, steel, red glass stones.
H 3.9 cm
Schmuckmuseum, Pforzheim

above
HUBERTUS VON SKAL
Der kleine Mann im Ohr, brooch, 1967
(The Little Man in the Ear)
Gold, plastic, steel. H 6 cm

right
HUBERTUS VON SKAL
Brooch, 1965
Gold, gilded iron, lapis lazuli. H 5.5 cm

DANIEL KRUGER
Neckpiece, 1977
Stones in silk with copper and silver.
L of largest pendant 6.8 cm
Schmuckmuseum, Pforzheim

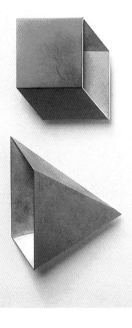

above
GIAMPAOLO BABETTO
Chain, 1972, and earrings, 1979
Gold. L of chain 32.6 cm; H of earrings 4.8 cm

left
GIAMPAOLO BABETTO
Brooches, 1976
Gold. Top H 4.8 cm; bottom H 5.8 cm

left
CAROLINE BROADHEAD
Bound cotton necklace, 1976
Cotton. L 66 cm
Crafts Council, London

below
CAROLINE BROADHEAD
Tufted bracelet, 1978
Wood, silver, nylon. Dia 10.5 cm
Shipley Art Gallery, Gateshead

right
CAROLINE BROADHEAD
Necklace and sphere bracelet, 1981
Woven nylon filament. Dia of necklace 22 cm;
Dia of bracelet 12 cm

left
DAVID POSTON
Three necklaces, 1974–75
Silver, hemp, cotton. L 13 cm, 30 cm, 35.5 cm
Crafts Council, London

below
SUSANNA HERON
Bracelet, 1971
Silver, resin. Dia 11 cm
Crafts Council, London

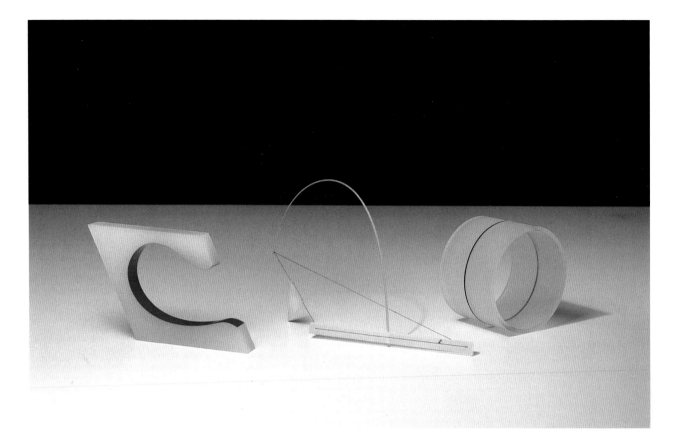

above, from left to right
SUSANNA HERON, PIERRE DEGEN, OTTO KÜNZLI
Bracelets, 1980
Nylon, acrylic, rubber. H of left piece 8 cm

right
SUSANNA HERON
Neckcurve, 1979
Acrylic, sprayed paint. W 22.5 cm
Crafts Council, London

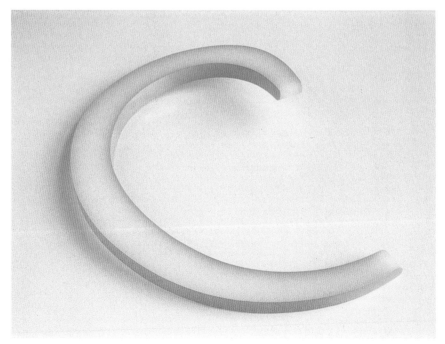

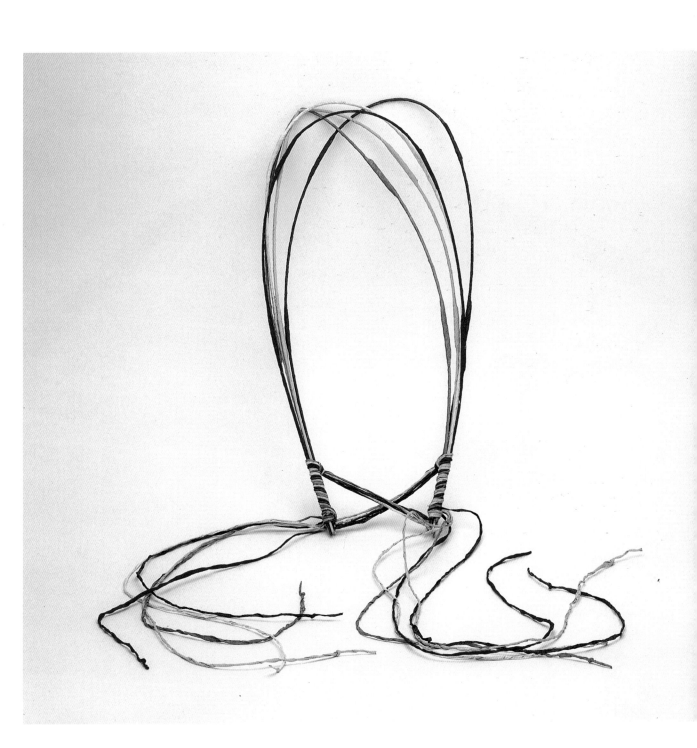

LAM DE WOLF
Neckpiece, 1982
Iron thread, textile, paint. H 115 cm
Stedelijk Museum, Amsterdam

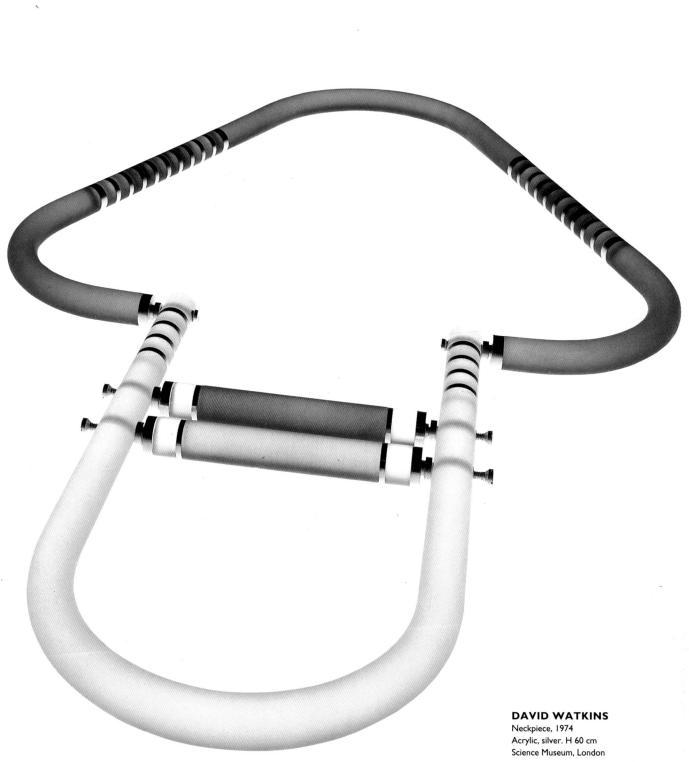

DAVID WATKINS
Neckpiece, 1974
Acrylic, silver. H 60 cm
Science Museum, London

right
JULIA MANHEIM
Three Rings, 1976
Silver, ebony. Dia c. 2.3 cm
Victoria and Albert Museum, London

above
OTTO KÜNZLI
Ring for Two, 1980
Steel. L 12.3 cm
Schmuckmuseum, Pforzheim

left
OTTO KÜNZLI
Gold Makes Blind, armband, 1980
Rubber, gold. Dia 8 cm

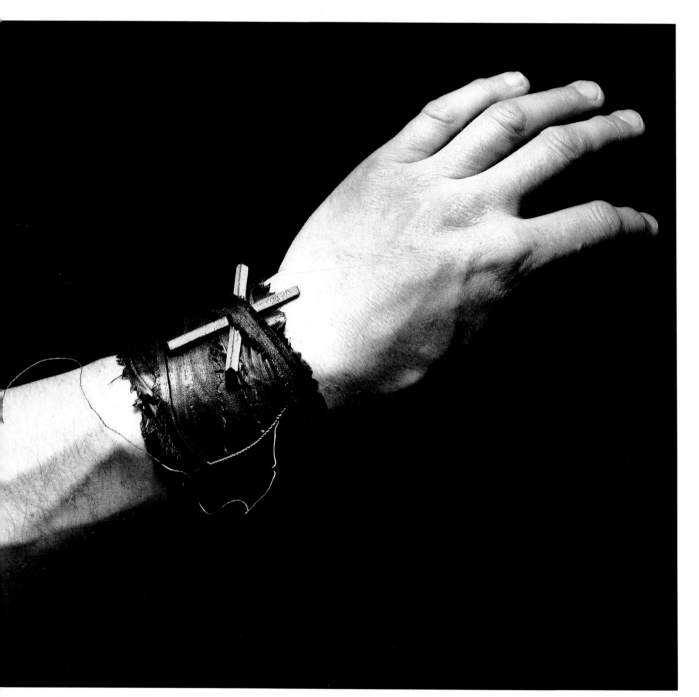

CHAPTER IV
IN PURSUIT OF SAVAGE LUXURY NOW

With deep-rooted prejudices jettisoned, jewelers at the end of the 20th century are free to explore ornament unencumbered and uninhibited. But with the impending 21st century, cultural and stylistic allegiances are more confused and uncertain, with social tensions reflecting a growing disparity between people.

Jewelry is gregarious. It is not conceived, nor does it function, in a vacuum, but monitors cultural, social and economic change. Hit by economic retrenchment, mainstream jewelry in the 1990s breaches few conventions but retracts to orthodoxy with lean ideas and artistic caution. But individual endeavour by some artist-jewelers contests this with new work of social relevance being produced.

In America, the 'European school' had established itself firmly and successfully, bringing about a reduction in ornate ornament. With its ardour cooled, new American jewelry flirted with 'good taste'. Rebecca Batal attended the Rhode Island School of Design (RISD) in Providence, the centre of jewelry production in the eastern USA. She studied under Louis Mueller, who had invited Otto Künzli to RISD for a teaching residency. Künzli's vision gave rise to some exceptional work from the students. He set an imaginative project: to make a piece of jewelry for a special friend or relative. This deliberately attempted to reverse the clichés of the Schmuckmuseum's 'Ornamenta' exhibition in Pforzheim in 1989, where goldsmiths were asked to create jewelry for 'famous personalities'. Batal's sensitive response at RISD produced a beautiful alphabet necklace of finely sawed lead letters for Bernard K. Waldropp, her poetry professor at Brown University. The intimate necklace looked comfortable on the bearded professor, yet it radiated excitement. The few pieces made by this talented jeweler all convey some sparse, subtle element of Surrealism.

Although Mueller's personal output plays wittily between conceptualism and late Pop, RISD has earned a reputation for producing jewelers with a leaning towards European 'conceptual' work (one reason, no doubt, for inviting Künzli). Three former students of Mueller – Sandra Enterline, Didi Suydam and Joan Parcher – provide further evidence of the school's more European approach. Parcher, who lives in Providence, cleverly utilizes the natural properties of materials. Using the transparent qualities of mica, she enjoyed the notion of creating jewelry out of stone. In 1991, she produced a series of Pendulum Pendants with soft graphite balls swinging across the torso to create smudge drawings on the wearer's garment. This concept was later developed in Holland by Dinie Besems, who used charcoal in a similar way, considering the residue as a symbol of transience.

Sandra Enterline, from San Francisco, and Didi Suydam, from Providence, make use of the aesthetics of exclusion and consistently produce refined, 'minimalistic' designs. This approach is also true of Claire Dinsmore, whose travels in Japan influenced her thinking. Free of embellishment, she uses the sensual, warm colour of copper, modestly folding, sewing and riveting informal expression into her jewelry. Impinging on our sense of touch, Lisa Spiros's carefully considered work is austerely

JOAN PARCHER
Pendulum Pendant, 1991
Graphite, steel wire. H 7.5 cm

THOMAS GENTILLE
Brooch, 1991
Eggshell inlay. H. 13.6 cm

uncompromising. Her jewelry provides a direct exposure to unblemished materials which engage us in an immediate sculptural experience with them. Spiros's acute sensitivity might owe something to Hermann Jünger, with whom she studied in Munich.

Minimalism was essentially an American art movement in the 1960s that rejected Expressionist devices. Yet several jewelers in the USA who arrived at these principles often did so through the influence of European goldsmiths – not only Jünger, but also Bury, Bakker, Watkins and Künzli. Although not Minimalists, their expression adapted itself well to 'discreet' ornament.

As we can see, jewelry's affinity with sculpture is a strong ingredient in the current creative debate. Joe Wood's concise work reflects his initial training as a sculptor. His jewelry has a directness, unburdened by tradition, which has evolved through an interaction between materials, processes and ideas. Wood's approach to constructions consolidates his sculptural vocabulary, which functions well within the parameters of jewelry.

While the alliance of goldsmiths is often to sculpture, enamelling requires a painter's sensibility. James Bennett, who started his career as a painter, has turned the difficult technique of enamelling to advantage by augmenting it with the more sculptural process of electroforming. His jewels are ambiguous, like fragments from an archaeological excavation, or fallen bosses from a cathedral's roof. The faded, matt colours of the enamel give the illusion of great age. Held in the hand, these lost, secretive heraldic amulets are surprisingly light in weight, which adds to their mystery. Mystery also surrounds the work of Sandra Sherman; a narrative documenting the finding of the components of her jewelry is hinted at, or reproduced, on its container. This narrative permeates her graceful, 'classical' interpretations, which transform fragments from old chandeliers, photographs and crushed glass, reinventing them into votive and ambiguous ornament.

Rachelle Thiewes lives in El Paso, Texas, perched on the Rio Grande on the US–Mexican border. Surrounded by wide open planes and hard spurs of spectacular mountain ranges, it seems unlikely that this arid landscape influences her work. Thiewes's eloquent interpretations of ornament create jewelry that oscillates and reverberates with sound. These clusters of forms are reminiscent of desert plants such as cactaceous pods, which of course are indigenous to her

RACHELLE THIEWES
Ring of Thorns, bracelet, 1995
Silver, gold, carved slate. Dia 15 cm

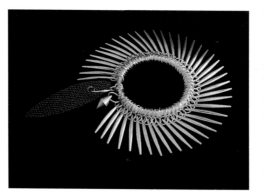

environment. Rachelle Thiewes is a teacher and also a collector of studio jewelry. Unlike many collectors, her home is not saturated with it; a few carefully selected pieces are placed through the house sensitively. Rarely have I seen jewelry look better in a domestic setting.

Breaking conventions is at the heart of the avant-garde, it is its raison d'être. Lisa Gralnick attacked conformity in the 1980s by abandoning gold. In the spirit of Modernism, her vision was worthy of architecture. Strong, unembellished forms in matt black acrylic resounded with the ethos of the De Stijl movement. Gralnick's stance was double-edged. Not only was this a protest against privilege, it was also her personal reaction to American studio jewelry with its 'ornament and self-indulgence'. In the 1990s, Gralnick returned to more traditional methods of working, exploring the 'non-neutrality' of materials and language by using precious and non-precious materials as well as texts. The materials and the language allow us an experience of both the past and the present, creating a dialogue and a possible conflict between our perception and interpretation of them.

Much has been made in these chapters of the democratic spirit of the modern jeweler. These challenges to convention are familiar in other areas of contemporary art too, but they are of particular relevance to jewelry because of its close associations with wealth. In America, we have seen some artist-jewelers attempting to challenge this privilege. For example, Fred Woell, Ken Cory and Bob Ebendorf replaced exclusive goldsmithing materials with ideas. Their Pop art imagery uses jewelry's obvious facility to carry messages. An offspring of this 'narrative' jewelry, with its strong rhetorical character, has become a vehicle for social, sexual and political issues. So much work, however, that purports to be politically and socially relevant, is justified by pepping up the content with explanatory texts and manifestos. The issues are often invisible in the works themselves. This is not to say, however, that all issue-based work is irrelevant – far from it.

Judy Onofrio, for example, recycles fragments of old costume jewelry, interweaving them with sumptuous glass beads. Her figurative work celebrates Pop culture with American heroes – presidents and cowboys – enshrined in 'corrals' as safe havens of retreat when the jewelry is not worn. This work refers back to the jewelry trade, glutinously gaudy and camp. Joyce Scott, also a sculptor taking on large-scale installations, uses beads, threading them into necklaces which confront social issues of racism and violence. But despite her awesome messages, there is a mood of optimism.

There is a glut of American work in this genre, much of it expressing wit and irony; but a large proportion favours an introverted, nostalgic approach with national fervour never far away. Bruce Metcalf from Philadelphia became a driving force in narrative jewelry, not only through his own idiosyncratic work, but through his

JUDY ONOFRIO
Splash Splash, brooch, 1992
Recycled glass beads, found objects. H 7.5 cm

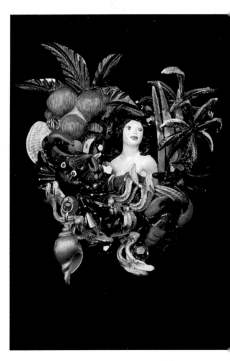

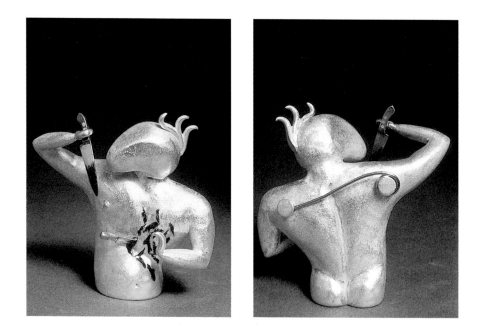

KEITH LEWIS
(front and rear views)
Just a Few Pricks, brooch, 1992
Brass, copper, silver-plated nickel, paint.
H 7 cm

writing, which often opposed the European domination of American jewelry. He also claims the status of artist for some American jewelers. In his essay, 'On the Nature of Jewelry', Metcalf writes: 'Many jewelers insist that their production be completely divorced from the marketplace. To some, jewelry has become a pure expression of thought and feeling, and less connected to the traditional values of ornament. Stripped of the familiar codes and functions, jewelry has become a modern art form.'

The core of this argument has long been exposed by artists who oppose systems of ownership and the commercialization of art, but for the jeweler it is a radical departure, though it is not without precedent. It might also be said that there are other jewelers whose work falls into Metcalf's artistic category but retains a semblance of commercial intent. Metcalf is, of course, talking of jewelry's conformity to commerce and the limits that this imposes on creativity. By implication, his argument is also a dig at jewelry's vast industry.

'Jewelry is meant to be worn. Unfortunately, it is more often locked away in safes, left to collect dust in drawers, hung on walls, kept languishing in collections or displayed in glass cases.' This hard-headed observation comes from the Austrian goldsmith, Peter Skubic. What indeed *is* jewelry for if not to be worn? One could adopt Bishop George Berkeley's theory that something exists only when it is perceived. But scepticism apart, Skubic has a point: most jewelry is made to be worn in society, scoring points for its wearer.

Keith Lewis, who was a pupil of Metcalf, is acutely aware of the triangular relationship which is generated between maker, wearer and viewer when jewelry is worn. Unlike some jewelers, especially men, he is brave enough to wear what he makes, and was struck by the social dislocations that occurred. Initially, his jewelry was formal and design-oriented, but grasping the subversive red rag principle, he launched himself into strongly emotive, figurative work. 'Figuration seemed to present a direct way to comment on human issues and dilemmas – a commentary that I believe to be infinitely more important (and satisfying) than formal explorations, which to my eye and mind are often conceptual fraud, created from an admixture of Freshman design principles, jargon and marketing.' The 'conceptual fraud' is perhaps a dig at the perceived idea of sanitized European influence on American jewelry, which Lewis and Metcalf oppose. Lewis's narrative expressions are very much his own, with messages that are often explicit yet not easy to decipher. But this is jewelry which pokes at the lazy eye in all of us. His concerns sometimes extend to his sexuality, confronting the raging assault of AIDS and the grief and loss that ensues. Thirty-five Dead Souls is a composition of pendants commemorating the friends Lewis has lost to AIDS. There is a thirty-sixth pendant, a gold bead hanging from a black string. It is a self-portrait.

Other narratives in American jewelry are articulated in a more escapist way. Betsy King, Thomas Mann and David Griffin are examples of this, as are Kim Overstreet and Robin Kranitzky from Richmond, Virginia, whose miniatures re-create childlike stereotyped fantasies. Overstreet and Kranitzky compose together at a large table, selecting from a room crammed with boxes full of ephemera. Their jewelry falls into a type of 'box-art' genre, transforming with alacrity found objects into their collages, which seldom stray from a Utopian vision of the surreal. Their jewelry is a crossover from assemblage art, which found its American champion in Joseph Cornell, who created magic worlds in boxes out of detritus. An artist of his calibre knew that assemblage or box-art had an instant appeal. But its very cuteness is seductive and can arouse suspicion.

Despite the clichéd view of America's West Coast as a Utopian shoreline for eccentric inventions, little of this dynamism seems to have found its way into studio jewelry in California. With some exceptions (some of which we shall look at later), what I saw there often confirmed Keith Lewis's 'conceptual fraud' theory: neat, clean and trouble-free. However, one cannot describe Ira Sherman's work in those terms.

Sherman lives in Denver, Colorado, where he produces Panaceas for Persistent Problems and Devices for Social Survival. These are his own titles, which describe the mechanized body sculptures that are a hybrid of his background: chemistry, mechanical engineering and goldsmithing. In an elegant curvilinear style, his contraptions verge on fantasies from science fiction. With a tongue-in-cheek whimsical philosophy, his 'wicked' work offers parodies of solutions for real human issues and dilemmas. For example, The Wrath of Persephone is a pneumatic anti-rape device, a chastity belt which unleashes darts on the penis of the unwanted intruder. Other inventions include The Pavlovian Trainer, used to curb verbosity, and The Arbitrator, his most recent, which is a two-person harness designed to solve deadlocked negotiations. It removes

IRA SHERMAN
The Arbitrator, 1995
Steel, stainless steel, brass, plastic, electrical components. H 152 cm

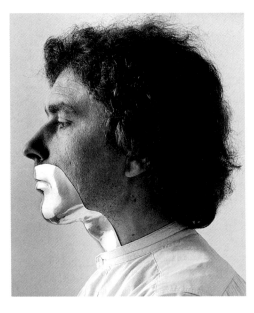

GEORG DOBLER
Brooch, 1993
Silver, steel. L. 11 cm

right
GERD ROTHMANN
The artist wearing Corner of One's Mouth,
1979
Silver. H 19.4 cm

inherent advantages one party may have over another, by forcing both into a prescribed period of time, set by a photoelectric egg-timer, to conclude talks, look each other in the eye and speak truthfully, while recording and documenting the terms discussed.

In Germany, the careers of goldsmiths soar. They bask in high esteem, with an assurance that manifests itself in their work. Manfred Bischoff, Georg Dobler, Daniel Kruger, Falko Marx and Gerd Rothmann are fine examples of this. At a time when jewelry, like architecture, is becoming increasingly international, their careers are models of individualism.

Daniel Kruger and Falko Marx disregarded conventional classifications of materials when creating their jewelry, transforming mundane and rare materials with resonance. Dispensing with their intrinsic values, gold, diamonds, iron, ink and sardine tins are magnificently democratized by Marx. Shards of shattered glass, splintered mirrors, pebbles and rare gems are chosen with meticulous eclecticism by Kruger. Yet neither of these men practise democratic principles in their jewelry. There is no party line or dogma to steer their thinking. There is also no real evidence of a consistency in style. Footloose and fancy-free, they both allow their imaginations to wonder, lifting any material or substance that takes their fancy. With no commitment to the present, they saunter through centuries of art, indulging where they will as if in some devilish ploy to confuse.

Perhaps such diverse work, particularly on Kruger's part, is an attempt to keep us guessing. This conjecture cannot be aimed at Manfred Bischoff, however, whose narrative style is immediately recognizable. His themes, for me, are often melancholic though they are open to everyone's interpretation. He writes: 'It's what the British writer, Bruce Chatwin calls a "Songline". These jewels are my songline, and perhaps someone will feel a sense of recognition.' Bischoff's figurative work is visually and technically complex with a purgative element running through much of it. A cathartic quality also pervades the structures of Georg Dobler, 'cleansing' the organic forms of nature by marrying them to synthesized geometry.

Transference is now central to Gerd Rothmann's work. Indeed, it could not be more so. Casting impressions directly from the body, he produces sensuous objects of beauty and ambiguity. Wrists, ears, noses, nipples and fingers are the more obvious sources for his investigations. But negative space is also explored – casting between fingers and indentations from within a clenched fist or buttocks. The gold castings are so fine and Rothmann's artistry so strong that the erotic overtones of this goldsmith's work are very powerful indeed.

The assurance and the consistently high standards that flow from the work of these German studios is impressive. Such assertion is also true of German goldsmiths whose sculptural interests have become endemic in their work as jewelers. Jens-Rudiger Lorenzen's career provides us with a lineage of such achievements, unencumbered by convention. Developing a personal visual syntax, his sculptural assemblages of metal and paper collage are highly wearable jewelry of character for either sex. These sculptural and moral concerns continue to run parallel in Elisabeth Holder's work but in the spirit of Modernism. The work of Rudolf Bott from Munich moves naturally between his interests in metalwork and jewelry, both contriving to build a strong sculptural vocabulary. In recent work one can detect a departure in his style to a freer, more deconstructive mode where metals are patinated and 'decomposed'. Jan Wehrens, also from Munich, was born and trained in Holland. He is

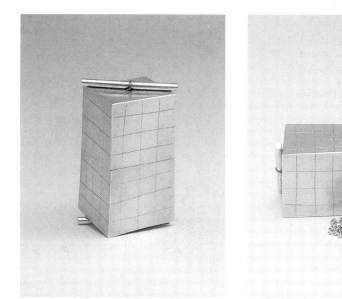

ELISABETH HOLDER
Divided Squares Revisited, 1994
Silver, steel, gold. H 12 cm

GRAZIANO VISINTIN
Brooches, 1994
Gold. Left 6.5 x 6.5 cm; above right
H 7.6 cm; below right Dia 8 cm

a prolific artist in sculpture and jewelry, weaned aesthetically on De Stijl.

A line of continuity runs through many artists' work, whatever the genre. We learn to look for it, searching it out for assurance like a touchstone. Yet occasionally an artist will interpret the flow and go off at a tangent. Giampaolo Babetto did just that temporarily, when he moved away from his spatial work to produce a series of emotive pieces of figurative jewelry. These were inspired by Jacopo da Pontormo's frescoes in the Certosa near Florence. Babetto had known this work from childhood and decided to interpret elements from it. With an élan and sensuality in keeping with Pontormo's painting, Babetto's jewelry expressed his personal response to this beautiful work. There have been many forays into fine art to fuel the goldsmith's imagination, but few have made the transition with such intelligence and sensitivity,

Giampaolo Babetto is now a positive influence in Italy with a career and persona that attracts many jewelers, several of whom attempt to ape his style. Of the younger generation, Graziano Visintin is strongly inspired by Babetto, yet retains an individualism. His idealism generates a dynamic expression, blending tradition with innovation. The distorted perspectives of Giorgio Cecchetto and Barbara Paganin also search for economy in volume with wry humour, fostering this new tradition in Italian goldsmithing.

Resistant to change, most studio jewelers in Italy work in gold. Consequently, there is not the forum for ideological arguments about precious and non-precious practices. Robert Smit, in Amsterdam, after years of self-inflicted exile from his workbench, returned to jewelry in the mid-1980s to emerge as Holland's principle activist in the use of high carat gold. His expressionistic work today thrashes gold about as liberally as Pollock did paint. Colour pigments are broadly applied to the precious metal in a tactile, painterly way, stressing the sculptural qualities of the pieces and emphasizing the value of contrasts. Gold, in rich coloration, is bent, beaten and abused in a symbolic denial of its status. So loose and free are these spontaneous works that the intrinsic value falls away as the jewelry's compelling beauty takes hold. A degree of irony pervades Smit's work, as it did that of Marian Herbst. Coming from a different source, her last group of provocative work, with its lively, kitschy interplay between the good and the gaudy, ran amok through Dutch sensitivities, sadly for the last time.

Studio jewelry is now more often esoteric in its eclecticism with talk of global vision and multiculturalism diversifying the arts. Ritual and customs from other cultures infuse the work of Trui Verdegaal, Jacomyn van den Donk and Lucy Sarneel.

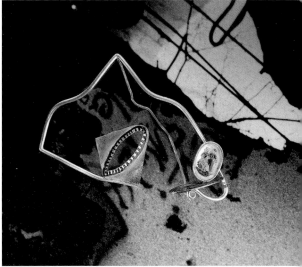

MARION HERBST
Brooch, 1993
Painted silver and brass. H 9 cm

WENDY RAMSHAW
Wendy Ramshaw wearing Calculator, 1995
White gold, cubic zirconium, fused silica glass,
perspex with resin inlay. H 33 cm

Sarneel deals with a broad range of issues sometimes interpreted in a narrative symbolic style. Jacomyn van den Donk exploits the sensual properties of jewelry with systems and materials aimed to excite our sense of touch. Like the earlier work of David Poston and Rachelle Thiewes, van den Donk's work is primarily for the wearer rather than the observer. With prudence, Trui Verdegaal re-uses old jewelry, building collages with narrative content. In collaboration with Jos van Heel, an imaginative deconstructive fashion and jewelry project was realized. These were often reinterpretations of earlier dress styles, some of which emphasized the beauty of simplicity and frugality.

We touched earlier on the relevance of continuity in an artist's work. Van den Donk and Sarneel were both born in the early 1960s, yet already one can detect a line of thought developing through their work. Philip Sajet is ten years their senior, yet has no apparent aesthetic or thematic sequence cementing his oeuvre. His work is similar to that of Daniel Kruger in this respect; both share a boundless love of materials and ornament touched with melancholy. In Sajet, this mood is reflected in his titles: The Laurel Wreath, Deep Night and Cloud Chain. In his most famous piece, The Francis Bacon Necklace, Sajet recites the painter's memorable chagrin, re-creating the words in a finely made gold chain, grammatically punctuated with tiny diamonds: 'Man now realises that he is an accident. That he is a completely futile being. That he has to play out the game without reason. He thinks of life as meaningless. He creates certain attitudes which give it a meaning, while he exists, though they in themselves are meaningless.'

With the early death of Helga Zahn and the dispersal to pastures new of Caroline Broadhead, Pierre Degen, Susanna Heron, David Poston and Julia Manheim, much of British jewelry's leadership has been removed, leaving the structure unbalanced. As a result, the role-modelling rests mostly on the shoulders of Gerda Flöckinger, Wendy Ramshaw and David Watkins. But, with a fresh transfusion of mature energy, British jewelry has become once more elevated by Peter Chang, Thomas Eisl, Geoff Roberts and Andrew Logan, all of whom have stepped from outside into jewelry's arena.

Chang trained as a painter, and colour determined his approach to jewelry. He carves laminated resin and bonded acrylic, punching the colours of the spectrum with confidence and conviction. The semi-industrial technique of cutting, carving and polishing is both malodorous and dangerous. His forms are exotic and fleshy, appearing like amphibious creatures from the deep. Thomas Eisl was born in the Tyrol and settled in London in the 1960s. Like Chang, he has had no formal training in jewelry and also works effortlessly (or so it seems) with furniture, lighting and sculpture, all expressing an inventive daring. He is a perfectionist – nothing in his work is allowed unless its function can be justified. For example, a tiny inflated balloon with its neck stretched, becomes a fastening mechanism, as does an inflated black rubber

GAVIN FRASER-WILLIAMS
Brooch and earring, 1994
Gold, steel. L 5 cm and 1.5 cm

tube which secures an aluminium brooch. These logical solutions extend into all aspects of his work with humour and irony. Though aesthetically challenging, everything can be justified with no hint of pretence. Geoff Roberts's training as a printmaker and sculptor is forthright in his colourful, satirical expressions. His work cleverly balances bread-winning designs with volatile, experimental sculptural bodypieces. Andrew Logan, London's gay impresario, sculptor and jeweler, shares Roberts's love of burlesque with jewel-encrusted mirrored collages. His work and thirty-year career have become the glittering conduit for fantasies, flitting between Carmen Miranda and Jeff Koons.

Chang's, Roberts's, Eisl's and Logan's work intrigues people – their sheer, unlikely inventions entertain. This is also true of Hans Stofer, who shares an intuitive feel for materials, but extends this to include vegetation, creating basket-like structures designed to enclose fruit or nuts.

More formal British studio jewelry continues, although the ideas are often slight. The work of Gavin Fraser-Williams, a young Welsh graduate from the Royal College of Art, proves that this need not be the case. Marrying the spirits of Classicism and Modernism, he subtly reinterprets architectural structures – architraves and pediments – in an ongoing investigation. Carefully selecting these 'classical' elements, his gold brooches and pins are temporarily lodged in blocks of solid steel that act as sculptural pedestals for the jewelry when not being worn. Cynthia Cousens also shows a willingness to experiment, but with the forms of nature. The biomorphic shapes of pods, seeds, shells and wood are absorbed into her designs with quiet restraint. With an intuitive approach and a sound understanding of discreet ornament, her jewelry has earned her widespread recognition.

Deconstruction, originally a literary term, makes bare the way in which meaning is constructed, ultimately to challenge the notion of authorship and originality. When applied to jewelry, this attempt to make tangible an anti-aesthetic can be seen to distort the values and meanings of given opposites, such as beauty and ugliness, while

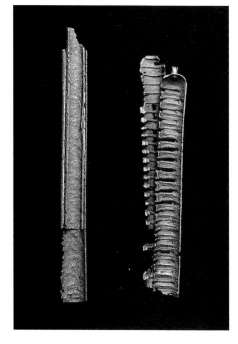

CHRISTOPH ZELLWEGER
Brooches, 1994
Cast steel. L 17 cm and 16 cm

often stretching materials to their limits. Its critique has been widely used, often pretentiously in the visual arts, to represent contemporary ills such as disorder, chaos, deprivation and social constraints. Not all jewelers whose work deals with socially and politically motivated issues would acknowledge this 'movement' as a source for their work, but it is loosely applicable to some.

'Goldsmithing is a middle class preserve, no wonder so much of it is safe and boring . . . too many jewelers look to the past for their ideas, we at least should try and face our own times and address its dilemmas.' This retort comes from Christoph Zellweger, a Swiss-born graduate from the Royal College of Art. Much of Zellweger's work addresses the fragmentation of society with eclectic references to events such as birth and death. In Chain, the symbolic imagery of technology and nature are joined together as life-giving forces, while the structure of the materials – latex and mild steel – give an illusion of decomposing. In the aftermath of Germany's reunification, Andrea Wippermann, Yvonne Galley, Inike Jorns and Ulrike Kleine (all from Halle, in former East Germany), produced equally powerful examples, demonstrating a not dissimilar assertive stance, with an armoured, almost brutal spirit of medievalism.

Some may describe studio jewelry, at the cusp of the new century, as being a kind of rich man's subculture. There is certainly less embarrassment about using precious materials now. The making process is often lengthy, so prices are rarely cheap. However, because of its beauty and unique malleable qualities, the impulse for using gold is strong.

'I would like some day to handle gold the way one handles plasticine.' This is Karl Fritsch from Munich, who, like Robert Smit, wishes to free gold from the burden of privilege. Re-using empty shanks from rings and frames from old brooches, Fritsch uses the lost wax technique and pours high carat gold into wax moulds in which the old jewelry is embedded. The amorphous gold shapes crudely and inertly grow out of the recycled jewelry, pushing their way sluggishly through the empty settings. Thus Fritsch creates a 'new unpretentious role for gold, overcoming our preconceptions and awe.' The results are often beautiful and witty with their casual disdain for elitism endorsing a freer approach to precious metals.

Despite Fritsch's unorthodox techniques, his training was rigorous, graduating from Munich's Academy of Art, where Detlef Thomas also studied. Thomas, however, is somewhat less impudent in his handling of gold. His work represents another conceptual aspect of jewelry, favouring an explicitness where the form of the work is determined by the idea rather than the materials. These often vigorous expressions have a sense of mangled chaos.

Patrik Muff took his revenge on the Modernist influence of his former teacher, Peter Skubic, with rigorous symbols of *memento mori*. Skulls, inscriptions, scrolls and ivy intertwine in elaborate tableaux. Thus, with Modernism exorcised, Muff launched himself into a eulogy of symbolism, principally between the polarized passions of love and hate, and between life and death. His stance against Modernism's models of cool restraint is assertive and almost aggressive. Aggression can be a powerful force for creativity and was the theme adopted by Wilhelm Mattar for his 'Arsenale: Aggression im Schmuck' (Aggression in Jewelry) exhibition in Germany in 1991. Confronted with Winfried Krüger's angry work, few might realize the hybrid of influences that are concealed between concept and execution. Dexterity is heavily camouflaged by his assertive painted symbols which erupt violently in his work.

There is also anger, turmoil and revolt against conservatism in Annamaria Zanella's jewelry. Hers is almost the only voice in Italy that harangues tradition: shards of glass and blackened iron attack the precious ramparts of Italian goldsmiths with all the tenacity of youth. Such strength is also found in Holland in Rian de Jong's diagrammatic woodwork, with surfaces left rough and sensual. Her work has been called capricious; objects to be handled, yet demanding to be worn, they never fully surrender their status as autonomous objects. Rian de Jong has worked with jewelry installations, as has Ruudt Peters, whose jewelry investigations span more than 20 years. He has said that 'Goldsmiths must be careful not to fall victim to the "nail-file syndrome" – they can deal masterfully with a space of one cubic inch, but they somehow become blind to larger, spatial contexts.' Peters's own installations and performances have become increasingly confident and imaginative. They engage our interest by focusing on jewelry's function and its presentation within the confines of a gallery space. In recent work he has used architectural elements as symbols of stability and tradition.

Some areas of exploration in the 1990s might be psychologically and morally questionable as jewelers edge towards a genre of barbarism and sadism. Following punks' love affair with razors and safety pins and gays' fetishistic devotion to body piercing and tattooing, dedicated practitioners of Body art now go to extremes of branding and scarification. But this sacrifice for adornment is hardly new. Past civilizations have used mutilation in the cause of more effective beauty. Some African tribes wore earrings so large that their earlobes dragged down in great loops;

RIAN DE JONG
Pendant, 1993
Wood. H 15 cm

SIMON FRASER
During performance of Alchemy with a Piano
at the ICA, London, 1993

right
SIMON COSTIN
Incubus, necklace, 1987
Copper, silver, glass, human semen,
baroque pearls. L 30 cm

multiples of gold hoops stretched necks to twice their natural length. There were the disc-lipped women of Chad and the fingernail cases worn by Chinese mandarins. Mutilation now, however, inhabits the hot zone for some contemporary jewelers with its 'kiss of fire'.

Simon Fraser and Simon Costin are jewelers with a reputation for the unorthodox. Fraser's Alchemy with a Piano was a twenty-four-hour performance at London's ICA, where a deconstructed upright piano was transformed into 200 pieces of jewelry. He has also created a series of rings that act as discreet ornament, but which change their meaning when adapted to double as branding irons. Costin's reputation soared when Scotland Yard's porn squad raided his Mayfair exhibition in pursuit of Incubus, a necklace of phials containing human sperm. This episode in turn prompted a commission from the Victoria and Albert Museum and numerous exhibitions followed. Drawing on his knowledge of dissection and taxidermy, the skin of reptiles, skulls, skeletons and the feet of guinea fowl are raw materials for his sensual work. Metaphysics and mythological literature provide his intellectual stimulus.

For uninhibited hedonists, undiluted sensual and sexual interpretations of jewelry are on the increase. Bernard Jongstra and Johanna Titselaar, known collectively as Gem Kingdom in Arnhem, Wolf von Waldow in Hamburg, Maria Hanson and Lyn Metcalf in London, all explore these possibilities through their work. Peter Hoogeboom also treads this fertile path with rituals of 'primitive' cultures inherent in the form and function of his jewelry. For his exhibition at Galerie Ra in Amsterdam, he focused his attention on healing with a collection of Mourning Chains. In a series of four, each represented a season of the year with fastenings for all to complete the annual cycle. Paul Derrez, the owner of Galerie Ra, is also a jeweler. His recent work, Body Tools (1995), responds to an aggressive homo-subculture in jewelry that is infused with eroticism. Robert Lee Morris was the former owner of ARTWEAR in New York. Included in the gallery's calender were two exhibitions with copious examples of jewelry's innate sensualism. With primordial sensibility, the Canadian Todd Tyarm brings pragmatism to his expressions. Prehistoric talismanic sharks' and horses' teeth, petrified eggs and flints are cradled in tautly woven leather pouches, which, when squeezed, release their ancient treasure. Rumanian-born Rolando Negoita builds jewelry and body pieces from brass, leather and drum skin, echoing the patina and oiliness of old engineering.

Bernhard Schobinger lives in Switzerland. Although outside the boundaries of our survey, his thinking is so central to our summing up of late 20th-century jewelry that it seems churlish not to include his contribution. As with many others, Schobinger's work is anti-elitist, relentlessly pursuing jewelry's independence from fashion and commerce. Like Karl Fritsch, he impudently 'abuses' gold by juxtaposing it with the unexpected – for example, necklaces of broken bottles, rough stones and

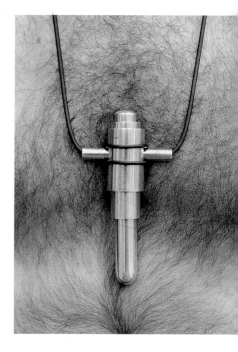

PAUL DERREZ
Pendant, 1994
Aluminium, rubber. L 11 cm

rocks of little intrinsic value. Social decline, chaos and human abuse are confronted in his traumatic expressions. He has said, 'I can no longer pretend harmony when the ugly has to be faced.' Such radical views raise questions about the perceived notion of the purpose of jewelry.

Jewelry still has a relevance in our society. Its ultimate business is unchanged, concerned as it always was with its unique facility to express emotions and to communicate – not least to communicate ideas, which have changed. Traditionally, jewelers have frequently attempted to pacify society, pandering to our needs with pretty, decorative designs. Jewelers now no longer have to do this. They can produce stronger, more relevant work which might address the dilemmas in society and by so doing, oppose them.

Otto Künzli, when summing up his response to the students at RISD in Providence, wrote, 'We jewelry-makers should open ourselves to the adventure and the power of the direct encounter between our jewelry and its wearer. But in order to do so, we need powerful, adventurous wearers: men and women who possess the desire, the will and the courage to open themselves up to us.'

Such courage exists – at least in packs. London's Cyberpunks bring together the fabric of new technology and discarded industrial waste. These are assembled and worn as ethnographic artifacts added to their nomadic dress style. With their war-painted faces, these posses of youth stalking the streets present a radical and inventive spectacle, and advance an awesome vision of the 21st century. Even the most radical expressions of change in jewelry appear manicured when compared to the raw, loud presence of this current street subculture. Yet the voices of dissent rising from these two groups are perhaps not so disunited.

DONNA NOLAN
Cyberpunk, London, 1991

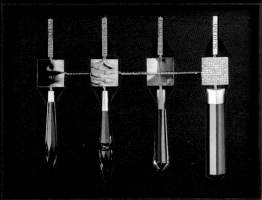

top
SANDRA SHERMAN
Lid of The Four Satisfactions box

above
SANDRA SHERMAN
The Four Satisfactions, diptych necklace, 1994
Sterling silver, photographs, glass, crystal. L 40.7 cm

right
REBECCA BATAL
Chain made for and worn by Professor Bernard K.
Woldrupp of Brown University, 1989
Lead, stainless steel. L 91.5 cm

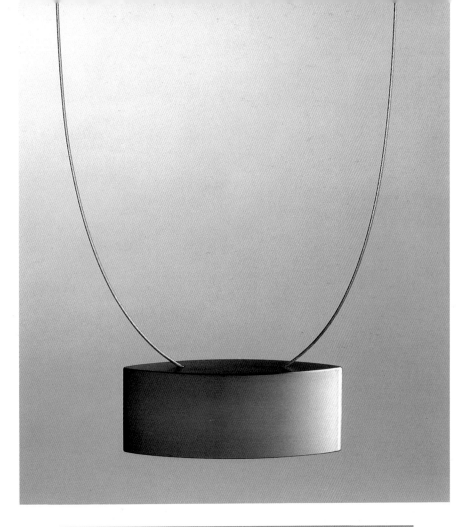

left
JOAN PARCHER
Brooch, 1995
Mica, sterling silver. L 9.5 cm

right, above
LISA SPIROS
Pendant, 1992
Stainless steel sheet and cable. W 6.4 cm

right
LISA SPIROS
Bracelet, 1992
Stainless steel mesh. H 6.4 cm

SANDRA ENTERLINE
Pendant, 1994
Sterling silver, oxidized. L 12.5 cm

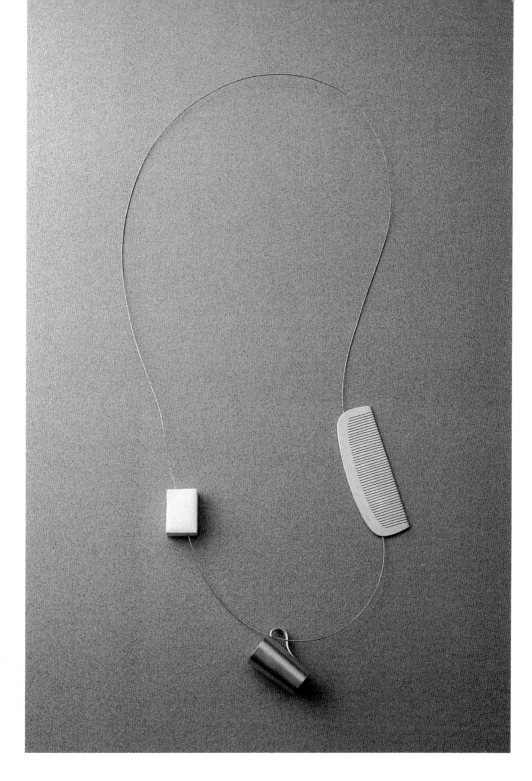

LOUIS MUELLER
Portrait of Marzee, necklace, 1988
Silver, enamel, steel. L 30.5 cm

left
JAMES BENNETT
Black Mark Neckpiece, 1994–95
Enamel, gold, silver, copper. L 14 cm

below
JAMES BENNETT
Brooch, 1994
Enamel, gold, copper. W 6.3 cm

right
LISA GRALNICK
The Tragedy of Great Love,
pendant, 1994
Sterling silver, gold, removable ring,
sugar, salt, glass (fabricated with
handmade chain), shown open.
H 4.5 cm

right
JOE WOOD
Three Scallop Brooches, 1995
Silver with burned oil patina, steel frame.
H 7.5 cm

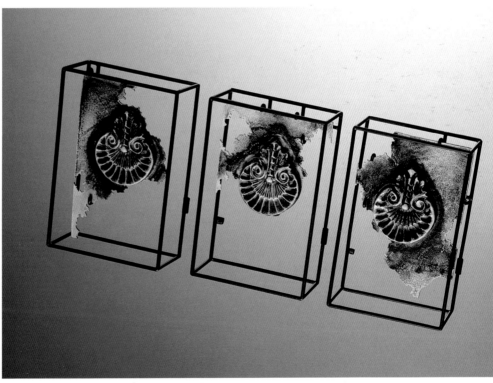

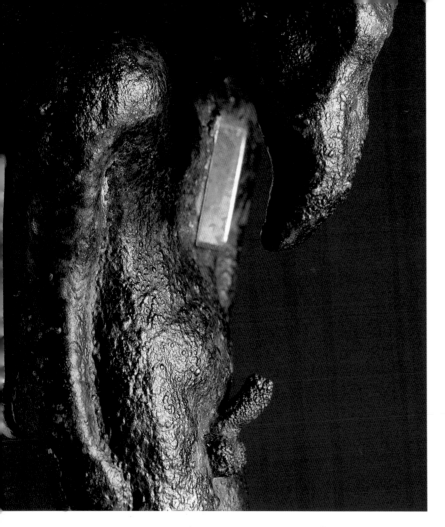

below
BRUCE METCALF
Catcher for a Young Icarus, 1994
Pins: silver, copper, gold, micarta.
Stage: wood, aluminium, brass, painted. H 3 cm

bottom
BRUCE METCALF
A Leaf as a Shelter, pin, 1992
Silver, copper. H 10 cm

above
KEITH LEWIS
Hanging Sad, pin, 1992
Copper electroform, sterling silver, gold, leaf,
verdigris. H 12 cm

96

JUDY ONOFRIO
Bracelet, 1995
Recycled glass beads. Dia 10 cm

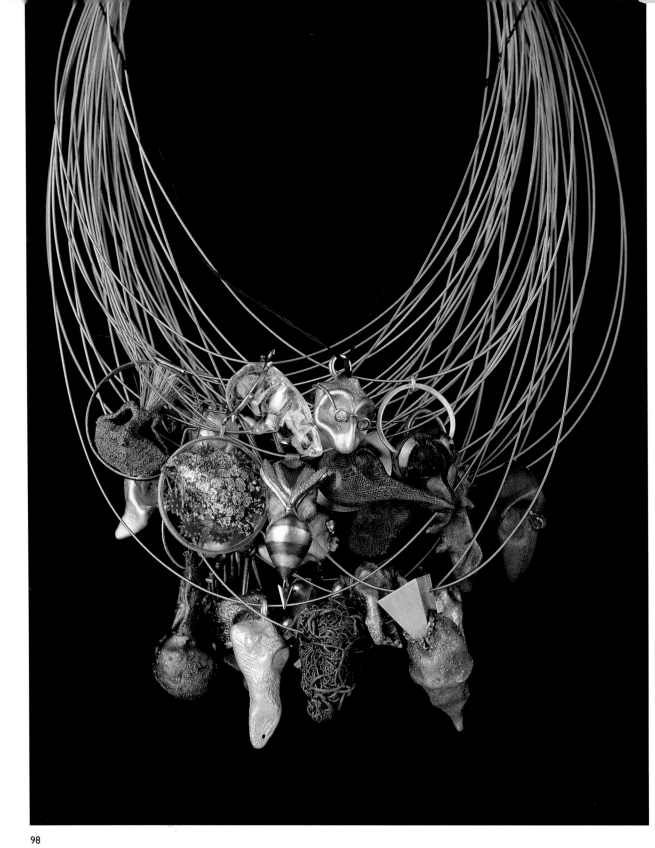

left
KEITH LEWIS
Thirty-Five Dead Souls, neckpiece,
1992–93
Assorted materials. H 26 cm

far left
DANIEL KRUGER
Brooch, 1995
Black stone, fire opals, gold.
L 7 cm

left
DANIEL KRUGER
Ring, 1995
Amethyst crystal, gold,
emeralds. H 6 cm

below left
FALKO MARX
Brooch, 1994
Iron, gold, platinum, diamonds.
W 7 cm

below
FALKO MARX
Ghost, brooch, 1992
Gold, water, ink. H 6 cm

JENS-RUDIGER LORENZEN
Brooch, 1995
Steel, silver, paper collage, varnish. H 5 cm

MANFRED BISCHOFF
Thomas Aquinas, brooch, 1989
Gold, silver, coral. H 9.5 cm

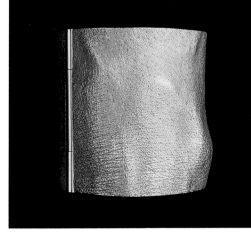

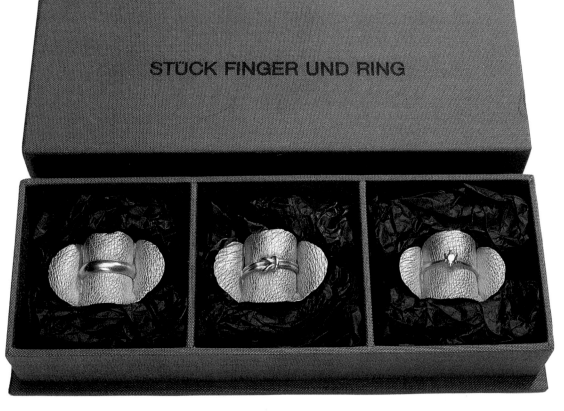

left
TRUI VERDEGAAL
Fashion and Jewelry Project, 1994
Dress and styling by Jos van Heel

above
RUDOLPH BOTT
Necklace, 1989
Silver. Dia 22 cm

103

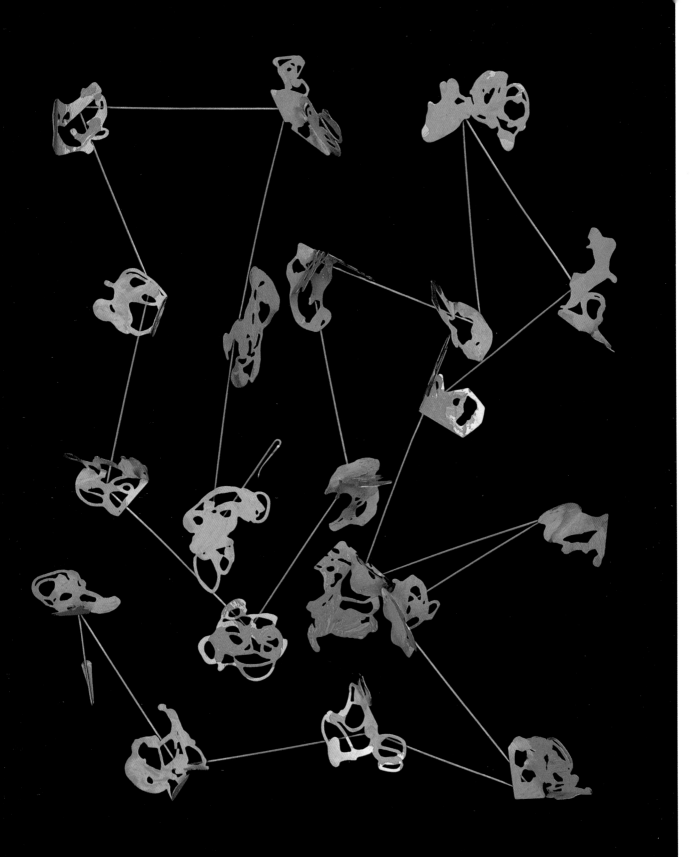

left
PHILIP SAJET
The Francis Bacon Necklace, 1992
Gold. L 100 cm

below
PHILIP SAJET
Splashes, necklace, 1994
Gold. W 40 cm

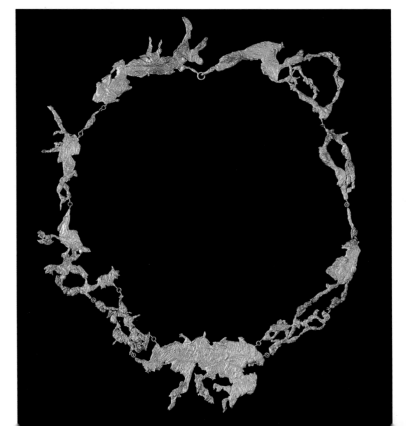

below
BARBARA PAGANIN
Anellidi, 1990
Gold, gold, silver plate. L c. 51 cm

inset
GIORGIO CECCHETTO
Ring, 1993
Gold. H 4 cm

right
THOMAS EISL
Brooch, 1994
Copper, inflated balloon.
H 12 cm

below
THOMAS EISL
Brooch, 1992
Aluminium, rubber tube.
H 10 cm

right
CYNTHIA COUSENS
Necklace Studies: Winter, 1993
Oxidized silver, textile, paper, twig.
L 107 cm

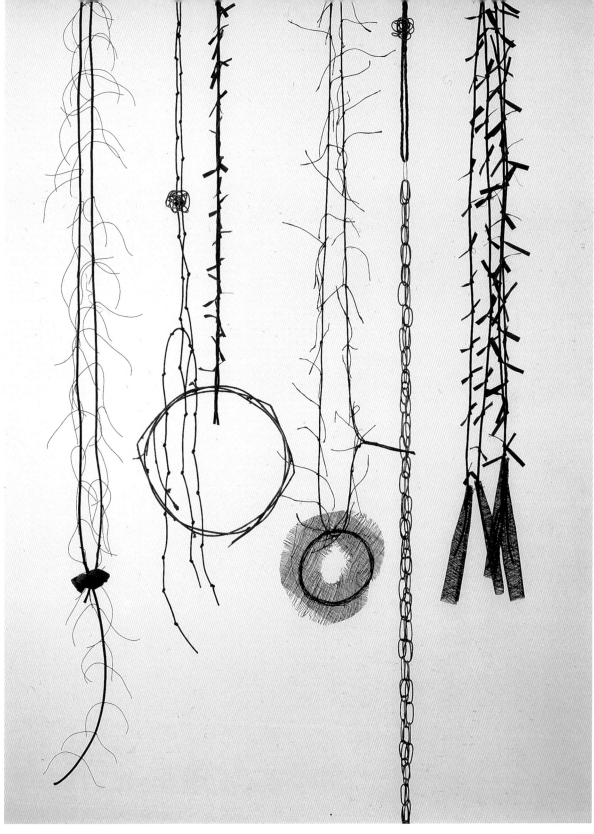

below
PETER CHANG
Bracelet, 1995
Acrylic, resin. Dia 18 cm

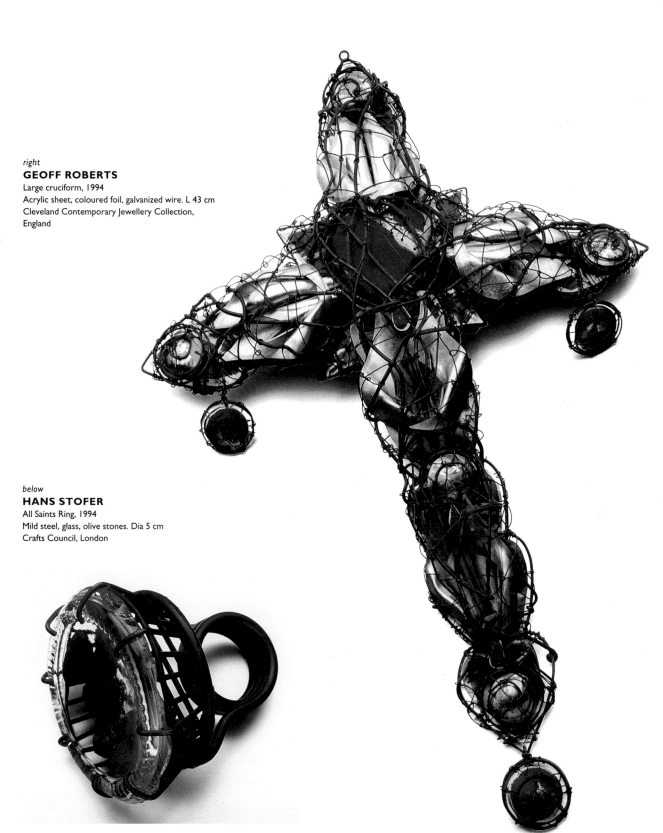

right
GEOFF ROBERTS
Large cruciform, 1994
Acrylic sheet, coloured foil, galvanized wire. L 43 cm
Cleveland Contemporary Jewellery Collection,
England

below
HANS STOFER
All Saints Ring, 1994
Mild steel, glass, olive stones. Dia 5 cm
Crafts Council, London

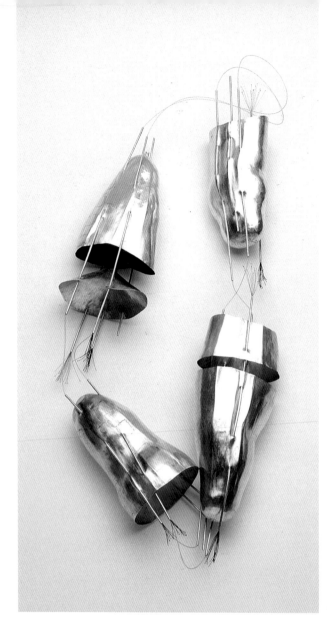

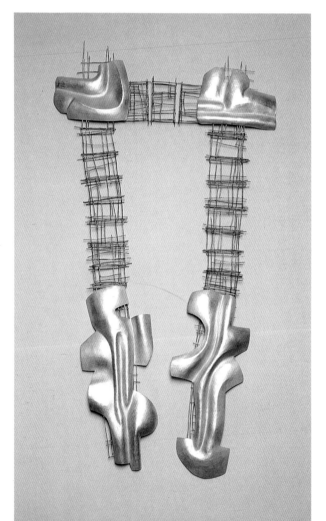

left
ULRIKE KLEINE
Birds, necklace, 1992
Silver. 40 cm

right
ANDREA WIPPERMANN
Neckpiece, 1991
Cast silver. L 26 cm

below
YVONNE GALLEY
Necklace, 1994
Silver. H 64 cm

left
CHRISTOPH ZELLWEGER
Chain (detail), 1995
Steel, latex. L 270 cm
Crafts Council, London

right (from top to bottom)
DETLEF THOMAS
Rings, 1994
Gold. H 6 cm; Dia 4 cm; H 6 cm

above
KARL FRITSCH
Brooches, 1993 and 1995
Gold. Longest piece 14 cm
Stedelijk Museum, Amsterdam (above right)

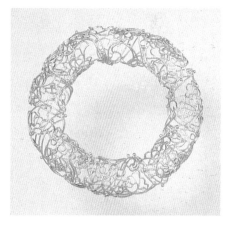

left
ANDREW LOGAN
Black Tiara and Latvian Leaps, necklace, 1994
Black glass, jet beads, grey pear-shaped stones.
H 30 cm and 21.5 cm

below
WINFRIED KRÜGER
Three brooches, 1991–92
Painted silver.
L of bottom piece 15 cm

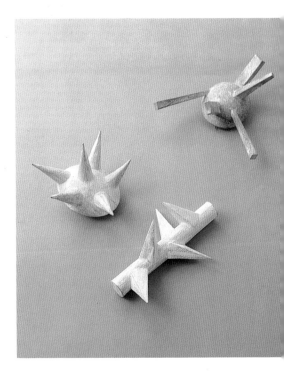

PATRIK MUFF
Brooch, 1989
Silver, amethyst, ivory. W 6 cm

above and right
RUUDT PETERS
Interno Installation at Horizonte,
Frankfurt, 1991

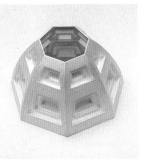

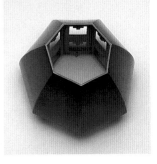

Interno Pantheon, brooch, 1991
Silver. W 6.5 cm

Interno Victoria, brooch, 1990
Silver. W 7 cm

Interno Terme, brooch, 1990
Silver. W 6.5 cm

ANNAMARIA ZANELLA
Brooch, 1992
Iron, enamel, glass, gold. L 6 cm

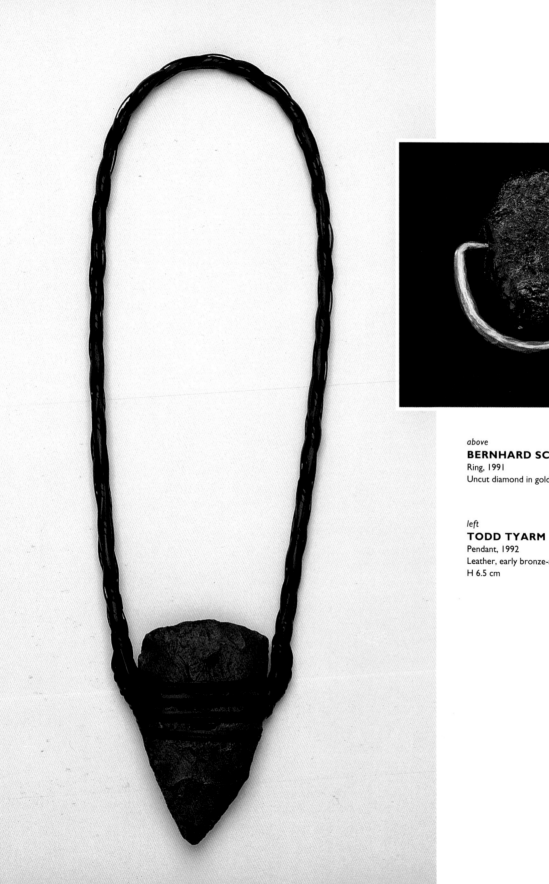

above
BERNHARD SCHOBINGER
Ring, 1991
Uncut diamond in gold. H 3 cm

left
TODD TYARM
Pendant, 1992
Leather, early bronze-age cutting tool.
H 6.5 cm

BERNHARD SCHOBINGER
Holiday in Cambodia, bracelet, 1990
Silver. H 8 cm

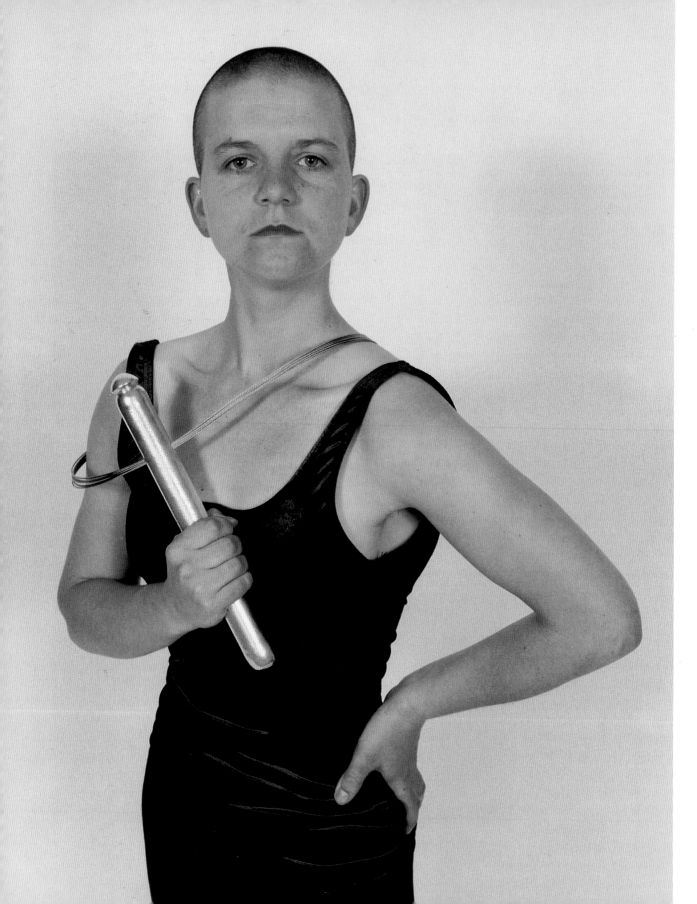

MARIA HANSON
Body Piece Five, 1993
White precious metal, stainless steel.
L 30 cm

PETER HOOGEBOOM
Mussel Cuff, 1989
Mussel shells, thread.
L 23 cm

Heavy Necklace, 1993
Stones, iron, glass cross.
H 2.5 cm

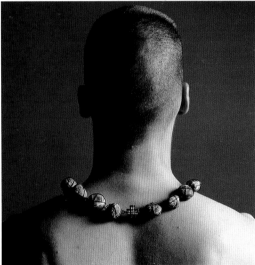

Love Harness, 1991
Leather, wood, glass, roses,
metal cross. H 14 cm

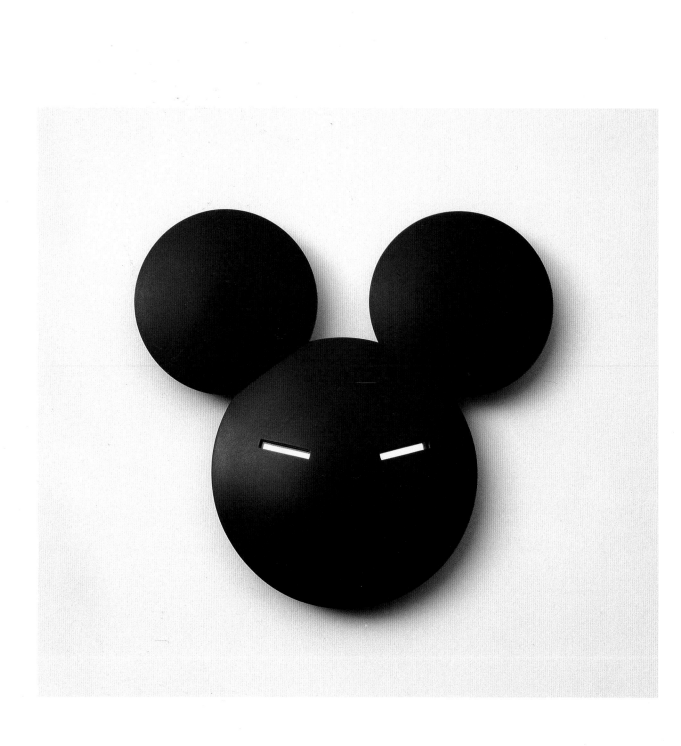

left
OTTO KÜNZLI
Mi, Myself and Eye, 1993
Acrylic, mirror glass. H 9 cm
Hiko Mizuno Collection, Tokyo

right
OTTO KÜNZLI
Three pendants from Cozticteocuitlatl
series, 1995
Silver, gold. *(from top to bottom)*
W 7.2 cm, 5.6 cm, 9.5 cm

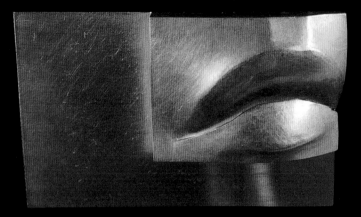

left

BRUNO MARTINAZZI
Mito/Logos, brooch, 1990
Yellow gold
W 7.2 cm

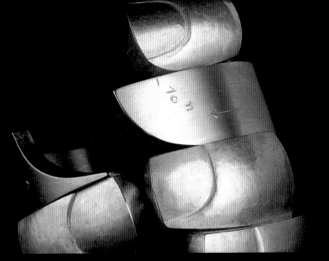

left

BRUNO MARTINAZZI
Metamorfosis, bracelet, 1993
Yellow and white gold. H 9 cm

below

HERMANN JÜNGER
Brooch, 1994
Gold. H 4.8 cm

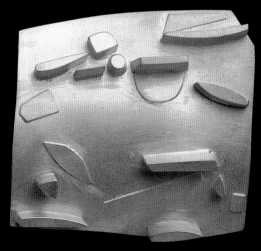

right
FALKO MARX
Ring, 1985
Gold, granulated diamonds.
H 3.1 cm

left
RUDOLF BOTT
Brooch, 1995
Gold. W 6 cm

GIJS BAKKER
Bullet, bracelet 1995
Steel. Dia 9 cm

BIOGRAPHIES

Collections listed below refer to collections of jewelry only.

ROBERT ADAMS (1917–1984)
British sculptor of non-figurative, constructed work of architectural scale, mostly in steel. During the 1950s he produced small quantities of jewelry, mainly in silver.

HANS APPENZELLER (b. 1949)
In 1969, with Lous Martin, he opened the first gallery in Holland to specialize in studio jewelry, later establishing a shop in New York (both now have their own outlets in Amsterdam). His own jewelry designs are based on the appeal of new, inventive ways of fastening.

Studied: Gerrit Rietveld Academy, Amsterdam

Collections: Museum Het Kruithuis, 's Hertogenbosch; Stedelijk Museum, Amsterdam

GIAMPAOLO BABETTO (b. 1947)
An important influence in European jewelry for over 20 years. Extolling the virtues of understatement, he creates jewelry of profound beauty and sculptural intensity. Like most Italian makers, he does not shy away from gold, yet it is the sculptural content that makes his work so striking. Lives in Italy.

Studied: Istituto d'Arte, Padua

Collections: American Crafts Museum, New York; Die Sammlung der Danner-Stiftung, Munich; Renwick Gallery, Smithsonian Institution, Washington; Royal College of Art, London; Victoria and Albert Museum, London

ULRIKE BAHRS (b. 1944)
Narrative, poetic expressions in jewelry, often confronting issues surrounding the human condition. Lives in Germany.

Studied: Akademie der Bildenden Kunst, Munich

Collections: Museum für Kunst und Gewerbe, Hamburg; Schmuckmuseum, Pforzheim

GIJS BAKKER (b. 1942)
Industrial designer, who, with his late wife Emmy van Leersum, brought Minimalism's cutting edge to Dutch jewelry design in the 1960s and 1970s. Intriguing investigations into jewelry continued through the 1980s and 1990s with characteristic wit and irony. Lives in Holland.

Studied: Amsterdam Academy of Art, Amsterdam; Kunstfack Skolen, Stockholm

Collections: Cleveland Contemporary Jewellery Collection, England; Museum Het Kruithuis, 's Hertogenbosch, Holland; National Museum of Modern Art, Kyoto; Power House Museum, Sydney; Stedelijk Museum, Amsterdam; Victoria and Albert Museum, London

REBECCA BATAL (b. 1967)
Produces powerful yet sensitive and wearable jewelry with subtle hints of irony. Lives in Boston, Massachusetts.

Studied: Rhode Island School of Design, Providence, Rhode Island

FRIEDRICH BECKER (b. 1922)
Pioneer of Modernist jewelry in the 1950s. He produced highly innovative kinetic pieces and work clearly informed by sculpture throughout the 1960s and 1970s. An influential teacher, he has received many distinctions and prizes. Lives in Germany.

Studied: Werkunstschule, Düsseldorf

Collections: Die Sammlung der Danner-Stiftung, Munich; Goldsmiths Hall, London; Schmuckmuseum, Pforzheim; Victoria and Albert Museum, London

JAMES BENNETT (b. 1948)
'I have consciously moved from procedural areas of enamelling such as cloisonné, in order to use enamel as a raw material, imperfect and sensual.' Bennett's ornamental language uses colour to elevate the seductive character of jewelry. He is Professor of Art at State University, New Paltz, New York.

Studied: State University of New York, New Paltz, New York

Collections: American Crafts Museum, New York; Art Gallery of Western Australia, Perth; Kunstindustrimuseum, Trondheim, Norway; Kunstmuseum, Oslo; Renwick Gallery, Smithsonian Institution, Washington; Royal College of Art, London

HARRY BERTOIA (1915–1978)
Successful designer whose sculptural concerns extended from furniture to jewelry, devising clever fastening solutions that became integral to the latter's aesthetic. Bertoia emigrated from Italy to the United States in 1930 and in 1942 joined Charles Eames, his contemporary at Cranbrook Academy, in California, where he developed designs for plywood furniture exhibited at the Museum of Modern Art in New York. In 1950 he began designing furniture for Hans Knoll on the East Coast, where, in 1952, he produced his famous steel rod grid chair.

Studied: Cranbrook Academy of Fine Art, Detroit

Collections: American Crafts Museum, New York; Musée des Arts Décoratifs, Montreal

MANFRED BISCHOFF (b. 1947)
Bischoff is a respected goldsmith with a unique creative spirit. A poetic narrative runs through much of his figurative style.

Studied: Fachhochschule, Pforzheim; Academy of Art, Munich

Collections: Museum Het Kruithuis, 's Hertogenbosch, Holland; Schmuckmuseum, Pforzheim

ONNO BOEKHOUDT (b. 1944)
His unique and unusual contribution to Dutch jewelry designs marries German influences and Dutch sensitivities. His working methods are integral to the visual vocabulary of his jewelry and sculpture. Lives in Holland.

Studied: Technical College, Schoonhoven; Staatliche Kunst und Werkschule, Pforzheim

Collections: Gemeentemuseum, Arnhem; Museum Het Kruithuis, 's Hertogenbosch; Powerhouse Museum, Sydney; Royal College of Art, London; Schmuckmuseum, Pforzheim

RUDOLF BOTT (b. 1956)
Goldsmith and silversmith. He brings to jewelry strong sculptural qualities by sensitive handling of surface textures. Not surprisingly, Bott, who lives in Germany, receives large-scale commissions for his work.

Studied: Zeichenakademie, Hanau; Akademie der Bildenden Kunst, Munich

Collections: Badisches Landesmuseum, Karlsruhe; Die Sammlung der Danner-Stiftung, Munich; Museum für Kunst und Gewerbe, Hamburg; Schmuckmuseum, Pforzheim

JOKE BRAKMAN (b. 1946)
Produces largely Minimalist and monochromatic concepts in jewelry using the transparency of materials for coloration and form. Now works with environmental installations. Lives in Holland.

Studied: Gerrit Rietveld Academy, Amsterdam

Collections: Museum Het Kruithuis, 's Hertogenbosch; Netherlands Costume Museum, The Hague; Stedelijk Museum, Amsterdam

CAROLINE BROADHEAD (b. 1950)
Broadhead's career was central to the development of jewelry design in the 1970s and 1980s. She invented compositions that presented personal ornament as part of the body, conveying intimate feeling rather than social status. Her work now involves installation and performance-based work, addressing issues of gender. Lives in London.

Studied: Leicester School of Art; Central School of Art and Design

Collections: Cleveland Contemporary Jewellery Collection, England; Contemporary Art Society, London; Gemeentelijkke Van Reekumgallery, Apeldoorn; Goldsmiths Hall, London; Israel Museum, Jerusalem; Shipley Art Gallery, Gateshead; Stedelijk Museum, Amsterdam

CLAUS BURY (b. 1946)
A major influence on both sides of the Atlantic for much of the 1970s. The changes he nurtured went far deeper than his choice of materials or even his

exceptional technique. The sculptural content of his expressions spoke a new language for the jeweler, drawing many young people to him. Lives in Germany.

Studied: Staatlichen Kunst und Werkschule, Pforzheim, under Reinhold Reiling

Collections: Deutsches Goldschmiedehaus, Hanau; Schmuckmuseum, Pforzheim; Victoria and Albert Museum, London

POL BURY (b. 1922)
His sculptures were activated by motors with clusters of balls or twigs clicking together, moving almost imperceptibly; his jewelry followed the same principles. Sets of editions were produced by Gem Montebello in Milan in the 1960s and 1970s.

ALEXANDER CALDER (1898–1976)
Jewelry was an integral part of the American sculptor's work. Inventor of the 'mobile', he trained as a mechanical engineer and attended evening drawing classes in New York in 1922. In the 1920s and 1930s he spent much time in Europe and experimented with motor-driven sculptures, but by 1932 most of his mobiles were generated solely by currents of air. Calder lived and worked mostly in France but also maintained a home and studio in Connecticutt.

Collections: Boston Museum of Fine Art, Boston; Musée des Arts Décoratifs, Montreal; Museum of Modern Art, New York; Victoria and Albert Museum, London; The Whitney Museum, New York

GIORGIO CECCHETTO (b. 1958)
Sophisticated modular constructions often distorting perspectives. Traditional geometrical gem stone cuts are sources for his witty pastiche compositions. Lives in Italy.

Studied: Istituto d'Arte, Padua

PETER CHANG (b. 1944)
Sophisticated and exuberant compositions in plastics with vivid, inventive use of colour. Lives in Scotland.

Studied: Liverpool College of Art; Slade School of Art, London

Collections: Crafts Council Collection, London; Contemporary Art Society, London; Helsinki Museum of Fine Arts, Helsinki; National Museum of Scotland, Kelvingrove, Glasgow; Victoria and Albert Museum, London

KEN CORY (1943–1994)
Developed a consistent graphic Pop art style throughout the 1960s and 1970s, using found objects and non-precious materials

Studied: California College of Arts and Crafts; Oakland College, California; Washington State University

Collections: American Crafts Museum, New York; University of Georgia; Washington State University

SIMON COSTIN (b. 1962)
Surreal and mystical inventions, achieved with imagination and unorthodox techniques such as dissection and taxidermy. He is currently researching designs for a 'suicide collar' with unstoppable mechanisms to choke the wearer to death. Lives in London.

Studied: Wimbledon School of Art, London

Collections: Kelvingrove Museum, Glasgow; Victoria and Albert Museum, London

CYNTHIA COUSENS (b. 1956)
Cousens's discrete interpretations of natural forms are expressed in subtle patterning and coloration. Her recent work shows a greater confidence in this approach. Lives in England.

Studied: Ipswich College of Art; Loughborough College of Art; Royal College of Art, London

Collections: Crafts Council Collection, London; Goldsmiths Hall, London

MARGRET CRAVER (b. 1907)
One of the first American artists to revitalize traditional jewelry techniques to express refined classical forms. She received international attention in the 1960s when she rediscovered a lost 16th-century enamelling technique, en resille.

Studied: University of Kansas; London School of Art; Worshipful Company of Goldsmiths

Collections: American Crafts Museum, New York; Boston Museum of Fine Art, Boston; British Museum, London; Newark Museum, Newark

SALVADOR DALÌ (1904–1989)
Leading member of the Surrealist movement, whose inventive designs extended to furniture and fashion – such as his designs for Elsa Schiaparelli, a dress adorned with a lobster and a hat in the form of a shoe. In the 1950s he created jewelry pieces that included a pulsating heart of rubies and dripping watches. Many designs for such works were taken from his paintings.

Collection: Minami Jewellery Museum, Kamakura, Japan; Owen Cheatham Foundation, New York

ALAN DAVIE (b. 1920)
Painter, goldsmith and jazz musician. Impressed by post-war American painting, particularly Jackson Pollock, his interests included 'primitive' art, myths and Zen Buddhism. His ornamental style in painting was well suited to the jewelry he made in the 1940s and 1950s to supplement his income. Lives in Hereford, England.

Studied: Edinburgh College of Art

Collections: Victoria and Albert Museum, London

GIORGIO DE CHIRICO (1888–1978)
Greek-born painter and a leading member of the Surrealist movement. Designed a small number of jewels for his wife during the 1950s. Some of his designs were executed by Masenza in Rome.

PIERRE DEGEN (b. 1947)
An orthodox training in jewelry provoked Swiss-born Degen to question jewelry's boundaries with little regard for goldsmithing traditions. His influence has been global. He is a teacher at Middlesex University in London.

Studied: Ecole des Arts Appliqués, La Chaux-de-Fonds, Switzerland

Collections: Cleveland Contemporary Jewellery Collection, England; Crafts Council Collection, London; Scottish Museum, Edinburgh; Shipley Art Gallery, Gateshead; Stedelijk Museum, Amsterdam

RIAN DE JONG (b. 1951)
Unrelenting sensual expression wrought in wood, metal and stone. Lives in Holland.

Studied: Gerrit Rietveld Academy, Amsterdam

Collections: Gemeentemuseum, Arnhem; Museum Het Kruithuis, 's Hertogenbosch; Stedelijk Museum, Amsterdam; Van Reekummuseum, Apeldoorn

MARGARET DE PATTA (1903–1964)
The leading pioneer of Modernism in jewelry in the USA. Rebelling against unimaginative conventions of commercial ornament, she originated stone cuts that widened the scope of transparent faceted stones, and that became an integral part of her sculptural reductivist designs. Although she trained as a painter and sculptor, she began making ethnically inspired jewelry in 1930, learning the basics of her craft from Armin Hairenian, an artisan. In 1940 she met Laszló Moholy-Nagy, whose School of Design she attended in Chicago in the same year until 1941. His influence led her to a vigorous application of Constructivist principles that transformed her approach to jewelry making. While at the 'Chicago Bauhaus' she met and married one of its design teachers, Eugene Bielawski, with whom she set up a jewelry studio in San Francisco's Bay Area in 1941.

Studied: San Diego Academy of Fine Arts; California School of Art; Art Student's League, New York; School of Design, Chicago

Collections: American Crafts Museum, New York; Musée des Arts Décoratifs, Montreal; The Oakland Museum of California, Oakland

PAUL DERREZ (b. 1950)
Designer of experimental jewelry in non-precious materials. New work explores homo-subcultural expressions. Founder of Galerie Ra, Amsterdam. Won the Françoise van den Bosch Prize in 1980. Lives in Holland.

Studied: Academie voor Industrielle Vormgeving, Eindhoven

Collections: Cleveland Contemporary Jewellery Collection, England; Museum Het Kruithuis, 's Hertogenbosch; Stedelijk Museum, Amsterdam; Tennen and Tennen, Amsterdam

CHARLOTTE DE SYLLAS (b. 1946)
De Syllas, born in Barbados, has a fundamental understanding of the nature and essence of the materials she uses, coupled with a painstaking devotion to acquiring skills. Symbolic messages are sometimes hidden in her commissions for the owner to discover.

Studied: Hornsey College of Art, Middlesex, England

Collections: Crafts Council Collection, London; Goldsmiths Hall, London; Victoria and Albert Museum, London

LAM DE WOLF (b. 1949)
Lam de Wolf's influential wearable work derives from her training as a textile artist; she develops her jewelry alongside her textile wall and floor pieces. Lives in Holland.

Studied: Gerrit Rietveld Academie, Amsterdam

Collections: Cleveland Contemporary Jewellery Collection, England; Museum Het Kruithuis, 's Hertogenbosch; Stedelijk Museum, Amsterdam

ROBERT EBENDORF (b. 1938)
A pioneer of creative expression in American studio jewelry, he devised ingenious alternatives for the goldsmith. Re-employing discarded materials, his early work in the late 1960s and early 1970s questioned the relevance of discreet conventional ornament. In later conceptual work he continued to reaffirm the value of a wide range of materials, imbuing them with renewed energy and special beauty.

Studied: University of Kansas; State School of Applied Arts, Oslo

Collections: American Crafts Museum, New York; Art Gallery of Western Australia, Perth; Art Institute of Chicago; Cooper Hewitt Museum, New York; Metropolitan Museum of Art, New York; Musée des Arts Décoratifs, Montreal; Museum of Fine Arts, Boston; National Museum of Design, New York; Oakland Museum of California, Oakland; Schmuckmuseum, Pforzheim; Victoria and Albert Museum, London

THOMAS EISL (b. 1947)
Self taught as a jeweler, logic and function are the mainstays of his idiosyncratic approach. He also produces furniture and lighting that are aesthetically challenging, while conveying a sense of humour. Born in the Tyrol, he lives in London.

Collections: Cleveland Contemporary Jewellery Collection, England; Crafts Council Collection, London

SANDRA ENTERLINE (b. 1960)
Jewelry made with economy of means and executed with clarity of thought. Lives in San Francisco.

Studied: Rhode Island School of Design, Providence, Rhode Island, USA

Collections: Oakland Museum of California, Oakland

ARLINE FISCH (b. 1931)
Research into the ancient cultures of South America and Egypt, as well as medieval Europe have provided Arline Fisch with the sound basis from which she works. She began making spectacular body ornaments early in her career; her later experiments in woven metal for neck, arm and head pieces were compiled in her book, *Textile Techniques in Metal for Jewellers*, a definitive manual for her inventive techniques. She is Professor of Art at San Diego State University.

Studied: Skidmore College, Saratoga Springs, New York; University of Illinois, Urbana; Kunsthandvaerkerskolen, Copenhagen

Collections: American Crafts Museum, New York; Art Gallery of Western Australia, Perth; Boston Museum of Fine Art, Boston; National Museum of Modern Art, Kyoto, Japan; Oakland Museum of California, Oakland; Renwick Gallery, Smithsonian Institution, Washington; Schmuckmuseum, Pforzheim; Victoria and Albert Museum, London

GERDA FLÖCKINGER (b. 1927)
Almost a lone pioneer of studio jewelry in Britain, producing concrete silver and enamelled compositions in the 1950s with Modernist motifs. Later her work became more florid with organic textured surfaces applied to rings, necklaces and earrings. Austrian-born, she emigrated to England in 1938 and was awarded the CBE 1991.

Studied: St Martin's School of Art, London

Collections: Crafts Council Collection, London; Goldsmiths Hall, London; Schmuckmuseum, Pforzheim; Victoria and Albert Museum, London

LUCIO FONTANA (1899–1968)
Fontana left Argentina in 1947 to settle permanently in Italy. He set about dismantling the boundaries between painting and sculpture, experimenting with his now famous slashed monochromatic paintings, a defiance that was echoed in his jewelry. He produced designs for sets of editions for Gem Montebello in Milan in the 1960s.

Studied: Brera Academy, Milan

SIMON FRASER (b. 1960)
Performance-based work and thematic collections of jewelry dealing with issues of gender, often humorously. Lives in London.

Studied: Sheffield City Polytechnic; Royal College of Art, London

GAVIN FRASER-WILLIAMS (b. 1966)
Finely made gold jewelry exploring Minimalist architectural elements, some composed with plinths. Lives in Wales.

Studied: Brighton Polytechnic; Royal College of Art, London

ELIZABETH FRINK (1930–1993)
British sculptor working mainly in bronze, of monumental human and animal figures. She made jewelry for friends.

Studied: Chelsea School of Art, London; Guildford School of Art, Guildford

KARL FRITSCH (b. 1963)
A new voice in German goldsmithing with informal and innovative use of precious metals often frugally recycling old jewelry settings. Lives in Germany.

Studied: Goldschmiedeschule, Pforzheim; Akademie der Bildenden Kunst, Munich

Collections: Die Sammlung der Danner-Stiftung, Munich

TERRY FROST (b. 1915)
Internationally renowned abstract painter. His painting is inspired by the Cornish sea and landscape and he has designed several pieces of jewelry, although some have never been executed. Lives in Cornwall, England.

ANTON FRÜHAUF (b. 1914)
During the 1950s he produced jewelry depicting stylized images drawn from Greek mythology. He later abandoned figuration and developed a vigorous abstract style.

Studied: Handelsakademie, Innsbruck; Academy of Art, Munich

Collections: Schmuckmuseum, Pforzheim

YVONNE GALLEY (b. 1966)
Sculptural spatial solutions to jewelry, with an integrity dependent neither on tradition nor modernity. Lives in Germany.

Studied: Burg Giebichenstein; Hochschule für Kunst und Design, Halle

THOMAS GENTILLE (b. 1936)
Meticulous transformations of non-precious materials into composed, Modernist jewelry. Evolving a unique combination of pure pigment inlay with eggshell, he creates his own refined, spatial compositions.

Studied: Cleveland Institute of Art, Ohio

Collections: American Crafts Museum, New York; Victoria and Albert Museum, London

LISA GRALNICK (b. 1956)

Gralnick's materials and techniques are as precise as her concepts. Her use of black acrylic in the 1980s challenged materials traditionally used in jewelry; her ambiguous juxtaposition of gold and steel contributes to the intriguing nature of her current conceptual work. Lives in New York.

Studied: State University of New York, New Paltz, New York

Collections: American Crafts Museum, New York; Boston Museum of Fine Arts, Boston; Stedelijk Museum, Amsterdam

MARIA HANSON (b. 1967)

Sculptural expressions in jewelry, some with undertones in weaponry.

Studied: Royal College of Art, London

WILLIAM HARPER (b. 1944)

One of the most innovative and skilful exponents of enamelling working in American studio jewelry. Mysterious and fantastic, his ambiguous creations often contain fetishistic undertones. Lives in Florida.

Studied: Western Reserve University; Cleveland Institute of Art, Ohio

Collections: Boston Museum of Fine Arts, Boston; Metropolitan Museum, New York; Renwick Gallery, Smithsonian Institution, Washington; Schmuckmuseum, Pforzheim

RENATE HEINTZE (1936–1991)

Born into a family of goldsmiths, her jewelry in the 1950s and 1960s retained symbolic elements of German folk tradition. She was later to evolve a more abstract and conceptual style informed by her interest in sculpture.

Studied: Goldsmithing apprenticeship with her grandfather; Institute for Artistic Craftsmanship, Halle

MARION HERBST (1944–1995)

Romping mischievously through a vast range of materials and disciplines, Herbst stood in the path of the thinking that influenced Dutch jewelry design in the 1960s and 1970s. Her colourful, witty and sometimes disrespectful experiments provided lively alternatives to the more logical expressiveness of the day.

Studied: Gerrit Rietveld Academy, Amsterdam

Collections: Cleveland Contemporary Jewellery Collection, England; Museum Het Kruithuis, 's Hertogenbosch, Holland; Stedelijk Museum, Amsterdam

SUSANNA HERON (b. 1949)

Major influence in new jewelry in the 1970s and 1980s. She produced a series of silver and resin jewelry with figurative and abstract designs. Finding the making process time-consuming and the market for her work too exclusive she changed medium and technique and made reductivist perspex and PVC collars and bracelets which more people could afford. In the early 1980s she developed nylon and painted papier-mâché 'wearables' – her term – which hovered between jewelry and dress. She now works as a sculptor and lives in London.

Studied: Falmouth School of Art, Devon; Central School of Art and Design, London

Collections: Cleveland Contemporary Jewellery Collection, England; Crafts Council Collection, London; Leeds City Art Gallery, Yorkshire; National Museum of Wales, Cardiff; Shipley Art Gallery, Gateshead; Stedelijk Museum, Amsterdam; Victoria and Albert Museum, London

ELIZABETH HOLDER (b. 1950)

An interest in engineering techniques brings highly inventive strategies to Holder's jewelry, which is impressive, not least for its continuity. Lives in Germany.

Studied: Staatliche Zeichenakademie, Hanau; Fachhochschule, Düsseldorf; Royal College of Art, London

Collections: Cleveland Contemporary Jewellery Collection, England; Crafts Council Collection, London; Goldschmiedehaus, Hanau; Museum für Kunst und Gewerbe, Berlin; Schmuckmuseum, Pforzheim

HERMANN JÜNGER (b. 1922)

Pre-eminent German goldsmith and influential teacher in Munich, whose career spans four decades. With superlative skills his work captures the spirit of spontaneity with fluid colourful expressions. Influenced by the painter Julius Bissier. Lives in Germany.

Studied: Staatliche Zeichenakademie, Hanau

Collections: Cleveland Contemporary Jewellery Collection, England; Die Sammlung der Danner-Stiftung, Munich; Goldsmiths Hall, London; Museum für Kunst und Gewerbe, Hamburg; Schmuckmuseum, Pforzheim; Victoria and Albert Museum, London

SAM KRAMER (1913–1964)

Known as Mushroom Sam, his wild jewelry wrought havoc on American sensitivities from the 1930s through to the 1960s. At the University of Southern California (from which he graduated in 1936) he attended a jewelry course run by the potter Glen Laken, whose open and liberating approach to art encouraged Kramer to make Surrealist jewelry. He returned to Pittsburg and worked briefly in the jewelry trade learning the rudiments of the craft. With his wife Carol, also a jeweler, he travelled to the Southwest to study Navaho jewelry, eventually settling in New York, in 1939, where he had studied gemology at the university. In the same year Kramer opened a shop on Eighth Street in Greenwich Village. Its eccentricity became well known and recognized for its bizarre promotions with advertising flyers, distributed by 'Space Girls' dressed in green tights and green make-up.

Studied: University of Pittsburg School of Journalism; University of Southern California; New York University

Collections: American Crafts Museum, New York; Musée des Arts Décoratifs, Montreal; Renwick Gallery, Smithsonian Institution, Washington

ROBIN KRANITZKY (b. 1956)

Kranitzky and Overstreet work together, producing surrealistic narrative jewelry. Both live in Richmond, Virginia.

Studied: Virginia Commonwealth University

DANIEL KRUGER (b. 1951)

Principal European goldsmith, born in South Africa, working idiosyncratically, independent of popular trends. He also works with ceramics. Lives in Germany.

Studied: Academy of Art, Munich; Michaelis School of Art, Cape Town, South Africa; University of Stellenbosch, South Africa

Collections: Die Sammlung der Danner-Stiftung, Munich; Institut für Auslandsbeziehungen, Stuttgart; Museum Het Kruithuis, 's Hertogenbosch; Schmuckmuseum, Pforzheim

WINFRIED KRÜGER (b. 1944)

Kruger's abrasive handling of metal creates jewelry invested with an urgent aggressive force. Lives in Germany.

Studied: Kunst und Werkschule, Pforzheim; Studien zur Kunst-geschichte an der Freien Universität, Berlin

Collection: Museum für Kunsthandwerk, Helsinki; Museum für Kunst und Gewerbe, Hamburg; Museum Het Kruithuis, 's Hertogenbosch; Schmuckmuseum, Pforzheim

OTTO KÜNZLI (b. 1948)

Swiss-born Künzli has been a major influence internationally, during the 1980s and 1990s, with conceptual work that subverts the values and traditions of conventional jewelry. He is Professor at the Akademie der Bildenden Kunst, Munich.
Studied: School of Art and Craft, Zurich; Academy of Art, Munich

Collections: Cleveland Contemporary Jewellery Collection, England; Die Sammlung der Danner-Stiftung, Munich; Museum für Kunst und Gewerbe, Hamburg; Museum für Kunsthandwerk, Helsinki;

Museum Het Kruithuis, 's Hertogenbosch;
Schmuckmuseum, Pforzheim

STANLEY LECHTZIN (b. 1936)
Lechtzin's interest in modern technology led him to
experiment with electroforming in the 1960s and to
create large yet lightweight work. His more recent
production methods have resulted from computer-
led technology. Lives in Philadelphia.

Studied: Wayne State University, Detroit;
Cranbrook Academy of Art, Detroit

Collections: American Crafts Museum, New York;
Goldsmiths Hall, London; Renwick Gallery,
Smithsonian Institution, Washington

KEITH LEWIS (b. 1959)
Subversive jewelry conceived intelligently,
confronting AIDS and other social and sexual issues.
Lives in Seattle, Washington.

Studied: Kent State University, Kent, Ohio

ANDREW LOGAN (b. 1945)
Logan's work and life urges us to follow the human
impulse to decorate and celebrate ourselves with
metropolitan glamour. Lives in London and Wales.

Studied: Oxford School of Architecture, Oxford

Collections: Andrew Logan Museum, Berriew, Powys,
Wales; The Arts Council of England; Cleveland
Contemporary Jewellery Collection, England

JENS-RUDIGER LORENZEN (b. 1942)
Strong sculptural elements in relief dominated his
jewelry in the 1960s and 1970s. More recently,
complex assemblages bonded in steel provide
impressions of harnessed energy. Professor at the
Fachhochschule für Gestaltung, Pforzheim.

Studied: Kunst und Werkschule, Pforzheim

Collections: Deutsches Goldschmiedehaus, Hanau;
Museum für Angewandte Kunst, Vienna;
Schmuckmuseum, Pforzheim; Royal College of Art,
London; Victoria and Albert Museum, London

JULIA MANHEIM (b. 1949)
Important figure in British jewelry in the 1970s and
1980s with work that questioned the role of jewelry
as a status symbol. From small-scale work in wood,
her style and material changed to large-scale body
pieces made from plastic-coated wire. She now
works as a sculptor and lives in London.

Studied: Hornsey College of Art, London; Central
School of Art and Design, London

Collections: Cleveland Contemporary Jewellery
Collection, England; Contemporary Art Society,
London; National Gallery, Victoria; Stedelijk
Museum, Amsterdam; Victoria and Albert Museum,
London

BRUNO MARTINAZZI (b. 1923)
Sculptor whose major influence in Italian goldsmithing
has spanned a career of 40 years. He depicts parts of
the body as eloquent symbols of the human condition,
focusing on concepts that address contemporary issues.

Studied: State School of Art, Florence

Collections: Die Sammlung der Danner-Stiftung,
Munich; Schmuckmuseum, Pforzheim; Victoria and
Albert Museum, London

FALKO MARX (b. 1941)
Principal German goldsmith transforming mundane
materials and augmenting them imaginatively with
gold into rich, exciting and witty collages.

Studied: Goldschmiedelehe, Fachhochschule, Cologne

Collections: Schmuckmuseum, Pforzheim

BARRY MERRITT (b. 1941)
Attention in the early 1970s focused on Merritt's
erotic fibreglass and enamel body works, such as
Deco Queen and Bullet Woman, which were later
followed by less overt sensual jewelry designs. Lives
in Georgia.

Studied: Rochester Institute of Technology; School
of American Craftsmen, University of Wisconsin;
Syracuse University

BRUCE METCALF (b. 1949)
For some jewelers, unleashed narrative expression is
forbidden territory. Metcalf treads its path raucously
and, like the Pied Piper, he has his followers. Lives in
Philadelphia.

Studied: Tyler School of Art, Philadelphia

Collections: American Crafts Museum, New York;
Cranbrook Academy of Art, Detroit; Musée des Arts
Décoratifs, Montreal; Philadelphia Museum of Art

PATRICIA MEYEROWITZ
British-born maker whose deployment of
Constructivist principles have dominated both her
jewelry and sculpture for over 30 years. She is also a
writer, and lives in New York.

Studied: Central School of Arts and Crafts, London

Collections: Victoria and Albert Museum, London

JOHN PAUL MILLER (b. 1918)
Miller's international reputation is derived from his
spirited application of granulation – the painstaking
technique of embellishing a gold surface with tiny
spheres of gold, some as small as $1/200$ of an inch in
diameter. His jewelry designs often derive from sea
and animal forms. Lives in Cleveland, Ohio.

Studied: Cleveland Institute of Art, Ohio; School of
American Craftsmen, Rochester

Collections: American Crafts Museum, New York;
Cleveland Museum of Art, Cleveland, Ohio;

Minnesota Museum, Minnesota; Renwick Gallery,
Smithsonian Institution, Washington; Texas State
College, El Paso, Texas

LOUIS MUELLER (b. 1943)
Mueller's jewelry is unashamedly concerned with
giving pleasure, openly and cleverly embracing
popular culture. Head of Jewelry and Light Metals,
Rhode Island School of Design, Providence.

Studied: Rhode Island School of Design, Providence

Collections: American Craft Museum, New York;
Museum of Art, Rhode Island School of Design,
Providence

PATRIK MUFF (b. 1962)
Death is celebrated in Muff's raucous jewelry,
characteristically populated with bones and skulls
that are sometimes placed secretively for the wearer
to discover. Lives in Germany.

Studied: Fachhochschule, Cologne

Collections: Schmuckmuseum, Pforzheim

RIET NEEVINCZ (b. 1925)
In the 1960s her work was influenced by her studies
in England where she was impressed by the sculptures
of Barbara Hepworth. Later her work became more
geometrical, with systematically arranged formal
compositions.

Studied: Arnhem Academy of Art; Apprenticed to
Professor Frans Zwollo; Central School of Art and
Crafts, London

Collections: Stedelijk Museum, Amsterdam

JUDY ONOFRIO (b. 1939)
Sculptor and jeweler whose raucous, American
repertoire is inspired by and regurgitates what
surrounds her. Lives in Minnesota.

Studied: Sullins College, Bristol, Virginia

Collections: Cooper-Hewitt Museum, New York;
Museum Het Kruithuis, 's Hertogenbosch; National
Council on the Arts, Washington; University of
Minnesota, Minneapolis

KIM OVERSTREET (b. 1955)
(see Robert Kranitzky)

Studied: Virginia Western Community College

BARBARA PAGANIN (b. 1961)
Clever use of grid structures, composed into crisp,
symmetrical jewelry, some of which is designed for
small production. Lives in Italy.

Studied: Academia de Belle Arti di Venezia; Istituto
Statale d'Arte, Venice

ALBERT PALEY (b. 1944)
Paley's status as an architectural ironwork artist has
almost eclipsed his significant contribution to

American studio jewelry in the 1960s and 1970s. The whiplashing lines and erotic undertones of his jewelry were in many ways a precursor of his sensual architectural commissions. Lives in Rochester, New York.

Studied: Tyler School of Art, Philadelphia

Collections: Boston Museum of Fine Arts, Boston; Metropolitan Museum of Art, New York; Philadelphia Museum of Art, Philadelphia; Renwick Gallery, Smithsonian Institution, Washington; Victoria and Albert Museum, London

JOAN PARCHER (b. 1956)
Conceptually based work that emphasizes a deep respect and appreciation of both mundane and exotic materials. Influenced by the sculptor Robert Culley and Hermann Jünger. Lives in Rhode Island.

Studied: Rhode Island School of Art, Providence, Rhode Island, USA

Collections: American Crafts Museum, New York; Renwick Gallery, Smithsonian Institution, Washington

EARL PARDON (1926–1991)
Painter, sculptor and teacher, whose most significant contribution to American art was his innovative jewelry. During the 1950s his use of structure in jewelry epitomized the decade's spirit of optimism with light, airy solutions to a more informal approach to adornment.

Studied: Memphis Academy, Memphis, Tennessee; Syracuse University, New York

Collections: American Crafts Museum, New York; Boston Museum of Fine Arts, Boston; Metropolitan Museum, New York; Musée des Arts Décoratifs, Montreal; Renwick Gallery, Smithsonian Institution, Washington

FRANCESCO PAVAN (b. 1937)
His linear, Modernist experiments revolve around themes of intriguing, sometimes flattened, perspectives. In the 1980s more 'painterly' surfaces gave way to dense grid structures which were woven into his work. An influential teacher, he is a major force in the Italian studio jewelry movement. Lives in Italy.

Studied: Istituto d'Arte, Padua

Collections: Die Sammlung der Danner-Stiftung, Munich; Schmuckmuseum, Pforzheim

RONALD PEARSON (b. 1924)
Silversmith and jeweler. His work in the 1950s and 1960s spanned production of hollow ware, jewelry and sculptural commissions. His deep commitment to jewelry contributed to the early success of Shop-One in Rochester, New York, which led him to take up numerous public appointments, including the board of America House in New York, a retail offshoot of the American Crafts Council. Lives in Deer Isle, Maine.

Studied: School of American Craftsmen, University of Wisconsin

Collections: American Crafts Museum, New York; Museum of Modern Art, New York; University of Rochester

RUUDT PETERS (b. 1950)
From reductivist strategies in the 1980s to mystic invocations and installations in the 1990s, Peters's energy and eclecticism has frequently scaled the boundaries of European goldsmithing. Lives in Holland.

Studied: Gerrit Rietveld Academy, Amsterdam

Collections: Museum für Angewandt Kunst, Hamburg; MOMA, New York; Royal College of Art, London; Schmuckmuseum, Pforzheim; Stedelijk Museum, Amsterdam

PABLO PICASSO (1881–1973)
Picasso modelled a number of medallions in terracotta that were later cast in gold. In the 1950s he designed a small number of jewels, some of which were made by the jeweler François Hugo.

MARIO PINTON (b. 1919)
Pioneer of studio jewelry in Italy in the 1950s, subtly reinterpreting the figuration of Egyptian and Etruscan imagery. His later style has focused on more abstract compositions. He has been a highly influential teacher.

Studied: Venice, Milan, and at the Villa Reale in Monza under the sculptor Marino Marini.

Collections: Die Sammlung der Danner-Stiftung, Munich

ARNALDO POMODORO (b. 1926)
Sculptor and goldsmith. He and his brother Giò brought international acclaim to Italian jewelry in the late 1950s and 1960s; their interpretations of Abstract Expressionism gave jewelry a new informality, encouraging other artists to explore jewelry as a form of art. Lives in Italy.

Collections: Schmuckmuseum, Pforzheim; Stedelijk Museum, Amsterdam; Victoria and Albert Museum, London.

DAVID POSTON (b. 1948)
Poston was born in the USSR and now lives in Northampton, England. As a reaction against jewelry symbolizing wealth and status, he became one of the first jewelers to use textiles in his work. He later applied the tactile nature of jewelry to well-proportioned forged iron and steel rings, necklaces and bracelets. He now works in education.

Studied: Hornsey College of Art and Design, Middlesex

Collections: Cleveland Contemporary Jewellery Collection, England; Crafts Council Collection,

London; Leeds City Museum, Yorkshire; Scottish Museum, Edinburgh; Shipley Art Gallery, Gateshead; Victoria and Albert Museum, London

JOHN PRIP (b. 1922)
One of the first American artists to be engaged by industry, designing flat ware, hollow ware and jewelry for production in the 1950s. The organic forms of nature and sea life found their way into his early jewelry design. His collaboration with Ronald Pearson and craftspeople Tage Frid and Frans Wildenhain in establishing 'Shop One' in Rochester set standards which were rarely to be matched. Lives in Reheboth, Maine.

Studied: Apprenticeship to Evald Nielsen, Copenhagen; Copenhagen Technical College

Collections: Museum of Contemporary Crafts, New York; MOMA, New York;

WENDY RAMSHAW (b. 1939)
Well known for her designs on the theme of variation, including multiples, notably rings that can be worn in different ways. Inventive and prolific, her work includes a collection using the traditional Wedgewood materials of jasper and basalt, and necklaces inspired by the late Picasso portraits of women. Awarded OBE, 1993.

Studied: Newcastle-upon-Tyne, College of Art and Industrial Design; University of Reading, England

Collections: Crafts Council Collection, London; Museum of Modern Art, Kyoto; Philadelphia Museum of Art, Philadelphia; Stedelijk Museum, Amsterdam; Victoria and Albert Museum, London

REINHOLD REILING (1922–1983)
Highly influential teacher and goldsmith whose career was dedicated to re-establishing the jeweler as a fine artist. His own work embraced Abstract Expressionism and later Pop and Conceptual art.

Studied: Kunstgewerbeschule, Pforzheim; Kunstgewerbeschule, Dresden

Collections: Die Sammlung der Danner-Stiftung, Munich; Goldsmiths Hall, London; Schmuckmuseum, Pforzheim

MERRY RENK (b. 1921)
Self taught as a jeweler, studied painting, sculpture and design at the Institute of Design in Chicago in the 1940s. Moholy-Nagy's influence can be detected in her carefully constructed designs. Later in her career she took to forging metals, producing more organic interlocking effects. Lives in San Francisco.

Studied: School of Industrial Arts, Trenton, Florida; Institute of Design, Chicago

Collections: Musée des Arts Décoratifs, Montreal; Objects USA, Johnson Wax Collection, New York; Oakland Museum of California, Oakland; San Francisco State College; University of Wisconsin

GEOFF ROBERTS (b. 1953)
The physical presence of his large-scale works challenges conventional notions of the size of most jewelry. His production pieces retain this integrity and receive strong interest from the fashion world. Lives in Scotland.

Studied: Birmingham College of Art; Royal College of Art, London

Collection: Cleveland Contemporary Jewellery Collection, England; Crafts Council Collection, London

GERD ROTHMANN (b. 1941)
Along with Bury and Maierhofer, Rothmann challenged the traditions of goldsmithing in the early 1970s with Pop art imagery in brilliant perspex colours. Within a few years he returned to gold, producing collections of conceptual work, much of which was not intended to be worn. This developed into his current preoccupation with skin and body castings in gold. Lives in Germany.

Studied: Staatlichen Zeichenakademie, Hanau

Collections: Die Sammlung der Danner-Stiftung, Munich; Museum Het Kruithuis, 's Hertogenbosch; Schmuckmuseum, Pforzheim; Stedelijk Museum, Amsterdam

PHILIP SAJET (b. 1953)
An unusual figure in Dutch goldsmithing, Sajet works with an eclectic choice of materials and techniques, producing collections of work that are equally as varied. Lives in Holland.

Studied: Gerrit Rietveld Academy, Amsterdam

Collections: Gemeentemuseum, Arnhem; Museum Het Kruithuis, 's Hertogenbosch; Stedelijk Museum, Amsterdam

MARJORIE SCHICK (b. 1941)
Since the 1960s Schick has made radical jewelry with strong, tense sculptural compositions. When not worn, these complex, colourful constructions evolve a formal, more orthodox identity. She is Professor of Art at Pittsburg State University.

Studied: University of Wisconsin, Madison; Indiana University, Bloomington; Sir John Cass School of Art, London

Collections: American Crafts Museum, New York; Applied Art Museum, Oslo; Cleveland Contemporary Jewellery Collection, England; Museum of Applied Art, Trondheim; National Museum of Modern Art, Kyoto; Renwick Gallery, Smithsonian Institution, Washington; Van Reekummuseum, Apeldoorn

BERNHARD SCHOBINGER (b. 1946)
Important influence in Switzerland whose powerful subversive and polemic jewelry pokes at the eye of convention. Lives in Switzerland.

Studied: Allgemeine Klasse Kunstgewerbschule, Germany

Collections: Kunstammlung der Schweizerischen Eidgenossenschaft, Switzerland; Landesmuseum, Stuttgart; Museum des Kunsthandwerk, Leipzig; Stedelijk Museum, Amsterdam

WILLIAM SCOTT (1913–1989)
Abstract painter inspired by the sea, landscapes and still lifes. He produced a small collection of jewelry mostly made in terracotta.

IRA SHERMAN (b. 1950)
Sherman creates body sculptures that are, in his words, 'Panaceas for Persistent Problems' – ironic, often parodic statements regarding the human condition.

Studied: University of Northern Iowa; University of Colorado

Collections: Byer Museum of the Arts, Evanston, Illinois; Hebner Educational Alliance, Denver

SANDRA SHERMAN (b. 1958)
Occasionally produces sequences that comment ironically on jewelry's traditions. Philosophical speculations also inform her work. Lives in Philadelphia.

Studied: Tyler School of Art, Philadelphia; Academy of Fine Arts, Munich

OLAF SKOOGFORS (1930–1975)
Olaf Skoogfors's family emigrated from Sweden to the USA before World War II and settled in Philadelphia. Influenced by Scandinavian and German work, his jewelry is European in spirit: cool, Modernist constructions that are well mannered and refined but that generate great energy and reveal a unique personal style.

Studied: School of American Craftsmen, Rochester, New York; Philadelphia Museum School of Art

Collections: Memorial Art Gallery, Rochester, New York; Museum of Contemporary Crafts, New York; Philadelphia Museum of Art, Philadelphia; Renwick Gallery, Smithsonian Institution, Washington

JILL SLOSBURG-ACKERMAN (b. 1948)
Jeweler and sculptor exploring dualities through personal ornament and installations. She is Professor of Art, Massachusetts College of Art, Boston. Studied: Tufts University, Boston

Collections: Cranbrook Academy of Art, Detroit; Massachusetts College of Art, Boston; Union Pacific Rail, New York

NAUM SLUTZKY (1894–1965)
Modernist jewelry and product design based on Bauhaus philosophy. He studied fine art and then engineering in Vienna, after which he worked as a goldsmith. He emigrated to England in 1932 and taught metalwork and engineering at Dartington Hall, Devon, and the Central School of Arts and Crafts, London, and the Royal College of Art, London. Appointed Head of School of Industrial Design at Birmingham College of Art and Craft.

Studied: Vienna Polytechnic

Collections: Museum für Kunst und Gewerbe, Hamburg; Schmuckmuseum, Pforzheim; Victoria and Albert Museum, London; Worshipful Company of Goldsmiths, London

ROBERT SMIT (b. 1941)
Smit has rained an assault on goldsmithing's traditions, with acrylic and computer-based work in the 1960s to a full-blooded return to gold in the 1980s, challenging the then widespread reductivist school of Dutch jewelry design. Lives in Holland.

Studied: Staatliche Kunst und Werkschule, Pforzheim; Technische School, Delft

Collections: Die Sammlung der Danner-Stiftung, Munich; Museum Het Kruithuis, 's Hertogenbosch; Schmuckmuseum, Pforzheim; Stedelijk Museum Amsterdam; Victoria and Albert Museum, London

ART (ARTHUR) SMITH (1917–1982)
One of the few black Americans to pioneer jewelry design in the 1940s and 1950s. His influences embraced biomorphic forms, marrying them to early African sculptural expression. Smith received a scholarship in the early 1940s to study the Cooper Union in New York. He became crafts supervisor at the Children Aid Society in Harlem, where he met Winifred Mason, a black craftswoman who made jewelry by recycling scraps of copper and brass. Under her influence he learned the rudiments of metalsmithing, working in her Greenwich Village shop for some years. On graduating from the Cooper Union in 1946 Smith opened his own shop and studio in Little Italy, but later moved to Greenwich Village.

Studied: Cooper Union, New York

Collections: American Crafts Museum, New York; Boston Museum of Fine Arts, Boston; Musée des Arts Décoratifs, Montreal; Objects USA, Johnson Wax Collection, New York; Walker Art Center, Minneapolis

ERIC SPILLER (b. 1946)
Jewelry in a Constructivist style for both women and men in steel, resin, acrylics and aluminium. Grid structures turned on the lathe or milled provide subtle Op art sensations. Professor of Faculty of Design, Robert Gordon University, Aberdeen, Scotland.

Studied: Central School of Art and Design, London

Collections: Aberdeen Art Gallery, Scotland; Cleveland Contemporary Jewellery Collection, England; Crafts Council Collection, London;

Goldsmiths Hall, London; National Museum of Modern Art, Kyoto

LISA SPIROS (b. 1959)
Central figure in new American jewelry, creating elegant and vigorous Minimalist concepts. Lives in New York.

Studied: State University at New Paltz, New York; Academy of Fine Art, Munich

CHRIS STEENBERGEN (b. 1920)
Pioneer of Dutch studio jewelry design in the 1950s when the work of Antoine Pevsner and Naum Gabo influenced his thinking. His work in the 1970s reflected the new Dutch style spearheaded by artists 20 years his junior.

Collections: Stedelijk Museum, Amsterdam; Ministry of Cultural Affairs, Amsterdam

HANS STOFER (b. 1957)
Recycling materials, Swiss-born Stofer came to jewelry in the 1990s, offering some fresh ideas with unexpected selections composed with elements of sculpture. Lives in London.

Studied: Qualified as an engineer in Switzerland; Zurich School of Art

Collections: Cleveland Contemporary Jewellery International, England; Crafts Council Collection, London

RACHELLE THIEWES (b. 1952)
Produces reductivist designs deliberately intended for either sex. She is Professor of Art at the University of Texas, El Paso.

Studied: Southern Illinois University, Carbondale; Kent State University, Ohio

Collections: American Crafts Museum, New York; Arkansas Art Centre, Texas; Art Institute of Chicago; University of Texas, El Paso

DETLEF THOMAS (b. 1959)
Earlier ordered structures were followed by symbols of mangled chaos, a development that attracted intriguing ambiguities to his thoughtful work.

Studied: Akademie der Bildenden Kunst, Munich

Collections: Die Sammlung der Danner-Stiftung, Munich; Musée des Arts Décoratifs, Paris; Royal College of Art, London; Schmuckmuseum, Pforzheim

TODD TYARM (b. 1961)
A contemporary creator of homages to prehistoric man. Lives in Canada.

Studied: San Francisco Art Institute, California

FRANÇOISE VAN DEN BOSCH (1944–1977)
The playful aspect of jewelry was an important

element in her reductivist designs, which pioneered the ideological democratic principles that pervaded Dutch work at that time. After her death The Françoise van den Bosch Foundation was established, promoting excellence in the field of international jewelry design.

Studied: Akademie voor Beeldende Kunst, Arnhem Museum, Amsterdam, 1990

Collections: Museum Het Kruithuis, 's Hertogenbosch; Stedelijk Museum, Amsterdam

JACOMIJN VAN DER DONK (b. 1963)
Exploring the tactile sensation of jewelry, her work has to be worn to bring the finely made 'chain' structures alive.

Studied: Gerrit Rietveld Academy, Amsterdam

EMMY VAN LEERSUM (1930–1984)
With her husband, Gijs Bakker, she became the most important influence in Dutch jewelry in the 1960s and 1970s. Her dedicated and disciplined attitudes pioneered a radical democratic approach to jewelry through an innovative, reductivist aesthetic.

Studied: Institut voor Kunstnijverhedsonderwijs, Amsterdam

Collections: Cleveland Contemporary Jewellery Collection, England; Museum Het Kruithuis, 's Hertogenbosch, Holland; Stedelijk Museum, Amsterdam; Victoria and Albert Museum, London

FRANS VAN NIEUWENBORG (b. 1941)
(see Martijn Wegman)

Studied: Academy for Industrial Design, Eindhoven

TRUI VERDEGAAL (b. 1965)
Frugal compositions made from recycling old jewelry with design concepts dependent upon found objects. Lives in Holland.

Studied: Gerrit Rietveld Academy, Amsterdam; Royal Academy of Plastic Arts, The Hague

GRAZIANO VISINTIN (b. 1954)
Coherent expressions in goldsmithing; wearers of the pieces are elevated by his finely tuned linear work.

Studied: Istituto d'arte, Padua

Collections: Die Sammlung der Danner-Stiftung, Munich; Royal College of Art, London; Schmuckmuseum, Pforzheim

HUBERTUS VON SKAL (b. 1942)
Czech-born, he is one of the most impressive European goldsmiths to have consistently produced work of a high calibre for 30 years. It is characterized by an informed interest in art and metaphysics. His exhibition installations are also memorable – for their beauty and surrealist content. Lives in Germany.

Studied: Akademie der Bildenden Kunst, Munich Schmuckmuseum, Pforzheim, 1989

Collections: Die Sammlung der Danner-Stiftung, Munich; Schmuckmuseum, Pforzheim; Victoria and Albert Museum, London

DAVID WATKINS (b. 1940)
Watkins's jewelry still carries the hallmarks of his training as a sculptor. Modernist in spirit, the scale of his work in the 1970s was generous and intended for the self-assured wearer. His prolific output in acrylic, steel and aluminium made him a figurehead of the avant-garde in British jewelry design in the 1970s and 1980s. He is Professor of Jewellery and Metalwork, Royal College of Art, London.

Studied: Reading University, England

Collections: Cleveland Contemporary Jewellery Collection, England; Crafts Council Collection, London; Goldsmiths Hall, London; National Museum of Modern Art, Kyoto; Schmuckmuseum, Pforzheim; Science Museum, London; Stedelijk Museum, Amsterdam; Victoria and Albert Museum, London

MARTIJN WEGMAN (b. 1955)
Frans van Nieuwenborg and Martijn Wegman started to work together in 1973, with materials and ideas new to jewelry at that time. Their concepts focused on the wearer, providing them with opportunities to change the shape or form of the work. They were later to move into product design. Both live in Holland.

Studied: Gerrit Rietveld Academy, Amsterdam

ED WIENER (1918–1992)
Wiener's jewelry, stylistically using familiar natural forms, captures in silhouette the structure of fish, shells, ovoids and the human figure. In 1945 he attended a crafts course at Columbia University and set up a studio at home. During the 1940s and 1950s he opened a number of retail shops in New York which became the focus for modern jewelry.

Collections: American Crafts Museum, New York; Musée des Arts Décoratifs, Montreal

ANDREA WIPPERMANN (b. 1963)
Provocative work that displaces and disconcerts our perception of jewelry's language. Lives in Germany.

Studied: Burg Giebichenstein; Hochschule für Kunst und Design, Halle

FRED WOELL (b. 1934)
One of the earliest exponents of Pop art in American jewelry in the 1960s. His keen sense of irony that informs his witty inventions shook the hallowed ground of goldsmithing and invaded the sensitivities of middle America. Lives in Deer Isle, Maine.

Studied: Cranbrook Academy of Art, Detroit; University of Illinois; University of Wisconsin

Collections: American Crafts Museum, New York; Georgia State University; New York State University; Renwick Gallery, Smithsonian Institution, Washington; University of Wisconsin

JOE WOOD (b. 1954)
Wood believes that the wearing of jewelry is an aesthetic act of collaboration between the artist and the wearer, the latter being part of the artist's intent. Lives in Cambridge, Massachusetts.

Studied: State Kent University

HELGA ZAHN (1936–1985)
Came to England from Germany and settled in London with frequent, prolonged visits to New York, where she had a studio. Her elegant and sophisticated designs of the 1960s and early 1970s pointed the way forward: unconventional graphic interpretations of natural forms were matched by an uncompromising sense of scale. Her early death robbed her of wider international recognition and public acknowledgment for her unique contribution to British jewelry.

Studied: Leeds College of Art; Central School of Art and Crafts, London

Collections: Goldsmiths Hall, London; National Museum of Wales, Cardiff; Schmuckmuseum, Pforzheim; Victoria and Albert Museum, London

ANNAMARIA ZANELLA (b. 1966)
Traditions and conventional materials are jettisoned – she uses glass and iron – and replaced by forceful yet highly wearable work, a phenomenon in Italian goldsmithing traditions.

Studied: Istituto d'arte, Padua; Academy of Arts, Venice

CHRISTOPH ZELLWEGER (b. 1962)
Born in Switzerland, but living in England, Zellweger produces work focusing on social issues as an alternative to mainstream jewelry.

Studied: Royal College of Art, London

Collection: Crafts Council Collection, London

LISTINGS
Museums, galleries, exhibitions and publications.
The exhibitions listed have been selected to represent a summary of each country's activity.

AMERICA
PUBLIC MUSEUMS AND GALLERIES

American Crafts Museum, 73 West 45th Street, New York, NY 10019
Established in 1955 as the Museum of Contemporary Crafts, it is the public face of the American Crafts Council.

Boston Museum of Fine Arts, 465 Huntington Avenue, Boston, Massachusetts 02115
Major international museum with important collections of fine and decorative art. Includes works by Alexander Calder, Margret Craver and Art Smith.

California Crafts Museum, Ghirardelli Square, 900 North Point Box 25, San Francisco, California 94109
Although the museum has no permanent collection, it provides a lively space for craft activities.

Cooper-Hewitt Museum, Smithsonian Institution, 9 East 90th Street, New York, NY 10019
Major collection of decorative arts and design, including some contemporary jewelry.

The Cranbrook Academy of the Art, Bloomfield Hills, Detroit, Michigan 48303-0801
One of the most prestigious and influential educational art institutions in the US, whose campus includes a museum with pieces by Bertoia, Eliel Saarined and Arthur Nevill Kirk.

Oakland Museum of California, 1000 Oak Street, Oakland, California 94607-4892
Collection of Californian art housing an impressive group of works by de Patta and other West Coast jewelers.

Philadelphia Museum of Art, PO Box 7646, Philadelphia 19101
Large collections of fine and applied art with jewelry by Harper, Skoogfors, Lechtzin, and Paley. Extensive exhibitions galleries.

Renwick Gallery, Smithsonian Institution, Pennsylvania Avenue at 17th Street NW, Washington DC 20560
Important national collection of US design and decorative arts with works by Mawdsley, Paley, Lechtzin and Woell and a programme of major exhibitions.

PRIVATE

Helen Drutt Gallery, 1721 Walnut Street, Philadelphia, Pennsylvania 19103
Promotes high-calibre work, particularly from jewelers and ceramicists from both America and Europe.

50 Fifty Gallery, 42 Stuyversant Street, New York, NY 10003
Lays emphasis on Modernist design, acting as a spur for the current revival in 1940–60s American applied art.

Jewelers Werk Gallery, 2000 Pennsylvania Avenue NW, Washington DC 2006
A lively gallery promoting international studio jewelry.

Sculpture to Wear Gallery, 9638 Brighton Way, Beverly Hills, Los Angeles, California 90210
A retail outlet which displays its contributors' work anonymously.

Susan Cummins Gallery, 12 Miller Avenue, Mill Valley, California 94941
Directed intelligently, the gallery presents an interesting programme of fine art and studio jewelry exhibitions mostly from US-based artists.

EXHIBITIONS
Selected list of American exhibitions published with catalogues.

1946 Modern Jewelry Design, *First National Exhibition of Contemporary Jewelry*, MOMA, New York

1948 *Second National Exhibition of Contemporary Jewelry*, Walker Art Center, Minneapolis

1955 *Third National Exhibition of Contemporary Jewelry*, Walker Art Center, Minneapolis

1959 *Fourth National Exhibition of Contemporary Jewelry*, Walker Art Center, Minneapolis

1962 *Young Americans*, Pasadena Museum of Art, Pasadena

1965 *Art of Personal Adornment*, American Crafts Museum, New York

1970 *OBJECTS USA*, American Crafts Council and tour

1970 *Goldsmith '70*, Minnesota Museum of Art, St Paul, Minnesota

1973 *Jewelry as Sculpture as Jewelry*, Institute of Contemporary Art, Boston

1974 *The Goldsmith*, Renwick Gallery, Smithsonian Institution, Washington

1975 *Forms in Metal*, American Crafts Museum, New York

1976 *Jewelry of Margaret de Patta*, Oakland Museum of California, Oakland

1977 *The Metalsmith*, Society of North American Goldsmiths, Phoenix Art Museum, Phoenix

1980 *Earl Pardon – Retrospective*, Art Gallery, Skidmore College, Saragota Springs, NY

1981 *Good as Gold*, National Museum of Art, Washington

1984 *Jewelry USA*, American Crafts Museum, New York

1987 *The Eloquent Object*, Philbrook Museum of Art, Tulsa, Oklahoma

1988 *10 Goldsmiths*, Rezac Gallery, Chicago

1989 *Robert Ebendorf – Retrospective*, Art Gallery, State University of New York, New Paltz

1989 *William Harper, Artist as Alchemist*, Orlando Museum of Art, Orlando, Florida

1990 *Arthur Smith – Retrospective*, Jamaica Arts Center, New York

1990 *Jewelries/Epiphanies*, Artists Foundation Gallery, Boston

1991 *Four Artists Reflect* (Ebendorf, Jacobs, Scherr, Scott), Society for Art in Crafts, Pittsburgh

1992 *Albert Paley, Sculptural Adornment*, Renwick Gallery, Smithsonian Institution, Washington

1992 *Todd Tyarm*, Artwear, New York

1992 *Crossroads*, Artwear, New York

1992 *John Iverson*, Artwear, New York

1993 *Rolando Negoita*, Artwear, New York

1993 *Robert Ebendorf*, Artwear, New York

1993 *The Art of Judy Onofrio*, North Dakota Museum of Art, Dakota

1994 *Brilliant Stories: American Narrative Jewelry*, USA Information Agency Tour

1995 *Messengers of Modernism, American Studio Jewelry 1940–1960*, Musée des Arts Décoratifs, Montreal, and tour

MAGAZINES

Ornament, P O Box 2349, San Marcos, California 92079-9806

Metalsmith, Society of North American Goldsmiths, 5009 Londonderry Drive, Tampa, Florida 33647

American Craft, American Crafts Council, 7 2 Spring Street, New York, NY 10012

BRITAIN
PUBLIC MUSEUMS AND GALLERIES

Birmingham Museum & Art Gallery, Chamberlain Square, Birmingham B3 3DH
National collections of fine and applied arts with modern jewelry by several leading British artists. Large temporary exhibitions galleries.

Cleveland Craft Centre, 57 Gilkes Street, Middlesbrough, Cleveland
An international collection of contemporary jewelry, developed since 1984 by Ralph Turner. The centre also boasts an impressive selection of studio ceramics. Both can be seen on application. Educational facilities.

Contemporary Applied Arts, 2 Percy Street, London W1P 95A
Founded in 1948 as the Crafts Centre of Great

Britain. it continues its role in stimulating excellence and making fine crafts available to the public.

Crafts Centre and Design Gallery, Leeds City Art Gallery, The Headrow, Leeds, LS1 3AB
Temporary exhibitions run alongside a continuous display of craftwork drawn from the UK with jewelry and ceramics predominant.

Crafts Council, 44a Pentonville Road, Islington, London N1 9BY
The national centre for the crafts, it presents a programme of high-quality contemporary and historical exhibitions in London, touring to many parts of the UK. Publishes exhibition catalogues and brochures as well as its own magazine, *CRAFTS*, and maintains two retail outlets; the one with its own headquarters in Islington, the other in South Kensington at the Victoria and Albert Museum. The Council's Collection includes some impressive modern British jewelry which can be seen on application.

Holburn Museum and Crafts Study Centre, Great Pulteney Street, Bath, Avon BA2 4DB
Permanent collection of 18th-century paintings and decorative arts. 20th-century fine crafts are sympathetically displayed and interpreted in the Crafts Study Centre. Occasional temporary exhibitions.

Midlands Art Centre, Cannon Hill Park, Birmingham, B12 9QH
Galleries, workshop facilities and bookshop with applied arts exhibitions.

National Museum of Wales, Cathays Park, Cardiff CF1 3NP
Multi-disciplinary museum housing international fine and applied art. Small group of modern jewelry by Zahn, Ramshaw and Susanna Heron.

Oriel, The Arts Council of Wales Gallery, The Friary, Cardiff CF1 4AA
Impressive exhibitions programme focusing on contemporary fine and applied art. Also maintains a large bookshop and national commissioning agency for designer-makers. Its gallery shop provides a high standard of craft work from across the UK.

Royal College of Art, Kensington Gore, London SW7
Influential art institution with important jewelry course run by David Watkins, who has acquired a small but distinguished jewelry collection. Visiting artists have included Babetto, Boekhoudt and Bakker.

Royal Exchange Crafts Centre, Royal Exchange Theatre, St Ann's Square, Manchester M2 7DH
A self-contained retail outlet within the theatre complex. Innovative displays promoting British crafts provide a broad spectrum of current activity.

Royal Museum of Scotland, Chambers Street, Edinburgh, EH1 1JF
International collections of decorative arts with extensive holdings of jewelry including contemporary work displayed in its own gallery. Works by David Watkins, Peter Chang, Breon O'Casey, Hermann Junger and Arline Fisch are included.

Ruthin Craft Centre, Park Road, Ruthin, Clwyd North Wales LL15 1BB
Scintillating outpost in rural Wales for the applied arts.

Shipley Art Gallery, Prince Consort Road, Gateshead, Tyne & Wear NE8 4JB
Has a national collection of contemporary crafts representing a broad range of disciplines. Active educational facilities.

Ulster Museum, Botanic Gardens, Belfast BT9 5AB
Multi-disciplinary museum with large collections of modern and applied art. Jewelry includes holdings from the Hull Grundy treasure and contemporary work from Irish and European artists.

Victoria and Albert Museum, Cromwell Road, London SW7 2RL
International museum with renowned collections of fine and decorative arts from 14th to 20th century. Substantial and impressive collection of jewelry on public display in the Jewelry Gallery with a small but interesting section devoted to contemporary work. Occasional jewelry exhibitions.

Worshipful Company of Goldsmiths, The Goldsmith's Hall, Foster Lane, London EC2
Established 800 years ago, the guild has provided 'mutual help and protection for the good of its fellows'. The Goldsmiths Hall stages exhibitions and conferences, and contains a fine collection of plate and jewelry.

PRIVATE

Argenta, 82 Fulham Road, London SW3
Well-established retail outlet for design-oriented jewelry.

David Gill Gallery, 60 Fulham Road, London SW3 6HH
A small, well-proportioned gallery with a programme focused mainly on innovative applied arts.

Electrum Gallery, 21 South Molton Street. London W1Y 1DD
Founded in 1971, this was the first commercial gallery for jewelry with an international exhibition programme.

Lesley Craze Gallery, 34 Clerkenwell Green, London EC1R 0DU
An energetic environment for British jewelers.

EXHIBITIONS

Selected list of British exhibitions published with catalogues.

1961 *First International Exhibition of Modern Jewellery*, Worshipful Company of Goldsmiths, Goldsmiths Hall, London

1963 *Modern British Jewellery*, Worshipful Company of Goldsmiths, Goldsmiths Hall, London

1966 *Friedrich Becker*, Worshipful Company of Goldsmiths, Goldsmiths Hall, London

1970 *Gerda Flöckinger*, Victoria and Albert Museum, London

1973 *British Jewellery*, Electrum Gallery, London, and tour

1973 *The Craftsman's Art*, Crafts Advisory Committee (now Crafts Council), London

1973 *The Observer Jewellery Exhibition*, Welsh Crafts Council, National Museum of Wales, Cardiff, and tour

1975 *Ten British Jewellers*, Crafts Council, London, Scottish Arts Council and Germany/Australian tour

1975 *Jewellery in Europe*, Crafts Council, London, Victoria and Albert Museum, London, and tour

1976 *Helga Zahn – Retrospective*, Crafts Council, London

1976 *Loot*, Worshipful Company of Goldsmiths, Goldsmiths Hall, London

1978 *Industrial Art of Gijs Bakker*, Crafts Advisory Committee (now Crafts Council), London

1980 *Susanna Heron, Bodywork*, Crafts Council, London

1980 *Tom Saddington, Jewellery Performances*, Arnolfini Gallery, Bristol

1981 *Caroline Broadhead*, Arnolfini Gallery, Bristol

1982 *Wendy Ramshaw*, Victoria and Albert Museum, London

1982 *Jewelry Redefined*, British Craft Centre, (now Contemporary Applied Art), London

1982 *Pierre Degen, New Work*, Crafts Council, London

1983 *The Jewellery Project* (Knapp Collection), Crafts Council, London

1983 *New Departures in British Jewellery*, American Crafts Museum, New York, and tour

1983 *Julia Manheim, Wire Wear*, Sunderland Arts Centre and tour

1984 *Cross Currents: Jewellery from Britain, Germany, Holland and Australia*, Power House Museum, Sydney

1984 *David Watkins*, Leeds City Art Gallery, Crafts Council, London

1984 *Modern Artist Jewels*, Victoria and Albert Museum, London

1984 *Ros Conway*, Victoria and Albert Museum, London

1984 *Patricia Meyerowitz*, Victoria and Albert Museum, London

1986 *Gerda Flöckinger*, Victoria and Albert Museum, London

1986 *Conceptual Clothing*, Ikon Gallery, Birmingham

1987 *New Spirit in Craft and Design*, Crafts Council Gallery, London

1988 *Contemporary British Crafts*, Museum of Modern Art, Kyoto

1989 *British Jewellery*, Crafts Council Gallery, London

1990 *Caroline Broadhead, Retrospective*, Crafts Council Gallery, London

1991 *Andrew Logan, An Artistic Adventure*, MOMA, Oxford

1991 *The 20th Anniversary Show*, Electrum Gallery, London

1994 *What is Jewellery?*, Crafts Council Gallery, London

1995 *Shining Through*, Crafts Council Gallery, London

1995 *Julia Manheim, The Shifting Emphasis*, Bury St Edmunds Art Gallery

1996 *Jewelry in Europe and America: New Times, New Thinking*, Crafts Council, London

MAGAZINES

Art Review, 20 Prescott Place, London SW4 6BT

Artists Newsletter, PO Box 23, Sunderland SR4 6DG

CRAFTS, Crafts Council, 44a Pentonville Road, London N1 9BY

GERMANY
PUBLIC MUSEUMS AND GALLERIES

Bayerischer Kunstgewerbeverein, Galerie für Angewadte Kunst Munich, Pacellistrasse 6-8, 80333, Munich
The headquarters of the Bavarian Craft Society with permanent collections and elegant rooms for temporary exhibitions. Two or three such shows a year – with excellent catalogues – are devoted to jewelry.

Cardillac Schmuckgallerie, Waldstrasse 56, 76133, Karlsruhe
Commercial gallery, owned and run by jeweler Cornelia Rating. Occasional exhibitons which will include a thematic series based on erotic work.

Danner-Stiftung Foundation, Thomas-Wimmer-Ring 9, 80539, Munich
One of the largest and most comprehensive collections of modern studio jewelry in Europe.

De Goldschmiedehaus, Altstadter Markt 6, Hanau am Main, 645
Established in the 1930s, with galleries equipped for staging temporary exhibitions mainly of goldsmithing and silversmithing.

De Hessichiches Landesmuseum, Friedenplatz 61, Darmstadt
Fine and decorative arts, with historical and modern collections and an excellent collection of Art Nouveau. Jewelry – including contemporary work – features prominently in the displays with well-presented exhibitions and authoritative catalogues.

Galerie Handwerkskammer, Max-Joseph-Strasse 4, Munich 803333
Large exhibition space staging exhibitions on craft and architecture with two or three shows a year devoted to jewelry or silversmithing, usually accompanied by well-documented catalogues.

Grassimuseum für Kunsthandwerk, Johannisplatz 5–11, 04103 Leipzig
National museum with extensive applied art collections and exhibitions, including modern jewelry.

Museum für Kunst und Gewerbe, 1 Steintorplatz, Hamburg 2
Large national collection of historical and modern applied art including some modern jewelry recording late 20th-century developments. Excellent exhibitions are staged including the long-awaited assessment of Naum Slutzky's work published with a fine catalogue in 1995.

Schmuckmuseum, Pforzheim im Reuchlinhous, Jahnstrasse 42, Pforzheim 753
The only museum devoted to the history of jewelry – from ancient civilizations to the present day. Prestigious international exhibitions are staged, often accompanied by scholarly catalogues.

Staatliche Museen zu Berlin, Preussischer Kulturbesitz, Kunstgewerbemuseum, Schloss Kopenick, D 12557 Berlin
National museum housing a large collection of applied arts with one of the most important reserves of studio jewelry from former East Germany.

PRIVATE

Galerie Matter, Luttigerstrasse 46, 5 Cologne 1
Promotes the goldsmith and the association, Forum für Schmuck und Design, which circulates information on studio jewelry's international activities through exhibitions, workshops and conferences. It also publishes an informative broadsheet.

Galerie Spectrum, Turkenstrasse 97, Munich D 8000
Long-established commercial gallery for jewelry with a reputation for staging well-considered exhibitions – usually solo shows concerning environmental issues.

Galerie Trykorn, Savignyplatz 13 Passage, 1000 Berlin 12
Focuses on internationally renowned goldsmiths, although they are sometimes supportive of new talent.

EXHIBITIONS

Selected list of German exhibitions published with catalogues.

1965 *International Ausstellung Schmuck*, Hessisches Landesmuseum, Darmstadt

1967 *Tendenzen '67 Schmuckmuseum*, Pforzheim

1972 *Jens-Rudiger Lorenzen*, Schmuckmuseum, Pforzheim

1974 *Claus Bury*, Schmuckmuseum, Pforzheim

1978 *Claus Bury, Hermann Jünger, Gerd Rothmann*, Hessiches Landesmuseum, Darmstadt

1979 *Otto Künzli*, Schmuckmuseum, Pforzheim

1981 *Ready Made*, Galerie Matter, Cologne

1982 *Reinhold Reiling – Retrospective*, Schmuckmuseum, Pforzheim

1983 *Otto Künzli*, Deutsches Tapetenmuseum, Kassel

1984 *Daniel Kruger*, Schmuckmuseum, Pforzheim

1987 *Wendy Ramshaw and David Watkins*, Schmuckmuseum, Pforzheim

1988 *Hermann Jünger – Retrospective* Schmuckmuseum, Pforzheim

1989 *Ornamenta 1* (major International survey) Schmuckmuseum, Pforzheim

1989 *Anton Cepka and Vratislar Novak*, Schmuckmuseum, Pforzheim

1991 *Aggression in Jewelry*, Galerie Matter, Cologne

1992 *Jan Wehrens*, Galerie für Angewandte Kunst, Munich

1993 *Schmuck Burg Giebichenstein 1970–1992*, Grassimuseum, Leipzig

1993 *13 Goldsmiths*, Bayerische Akademie der Schonen Kunst, Munich

1993 *Kunstoff Schmuck Kunst 1923–1993*, Galerie Biro, Munich

1993 *Gerd Rothmann*, Deutsches Goldschmiedehaus, Hanau

1993 *Ebbe Weiss Weingart Schmuck 1946–1993* Schmuckmuseum, Pforzheim

1993 *Renate Heintze*, Burg Giebichenstein, Hochschule für Kunst und Design, Halle

1995 *Naum Slutzky 1894–1965*, Museum für Kunst und Gewerbe, Hamburg

MAGAZINES

Art Aurea, Ebner Verlag, Karlstrasse 41, Postfach 3066 Ulm/Doyan 7900

Kunst und Handwerk, Postfach 8120 D4000 Düsseldorf 1

Gold und Silber und Schmuck, Konradin-Verlag, D7022, Leinfelden bei, Stuttgart

Goldschmiede Zeitung, Ruhlee-Diebener Verlag. Postfach 450, 7000 Stuttgart 70

HOLLAND
PUBLIC MUSEUMS AND GALLERIES

Het Van Reekummuseum, Koninginnelaan, 7315 BJ, Apeldoorn
National museum with important collection of art design and applied arts. Important in documenting jewelry during 1970s and 1980s.

Museum Het Kruithuis, Citadellaan 7, 5211 XA, 's Hertogenbosch
Museum of modern art with contemporary galleries. Fine selection of modern jewelry; some important jewelry shows have been initiated here.

Stedelijk Museum, Paulus Porerstraat 13, 1071 CX, Amsterdam
International museum of modern art, with collections of design and applied arts. A number of important jewelry exhibitions have been staged over the past thirty years; large international collection of modern jewelry with emphasis on Dutch design.

PRIVATE

Galerie Carin Delcourt van Krimpen, Fokke Simonszsztraat 8, 1017 TG, Amsterdam
A gallery specializing in jewelry with an eclectic exhibitions programme of ethnographic, antique and contemporary designs.

Galerie Louise Smit, Prinsengracht 615, 1016 HT, Amsterdam
Specializing in fine goldsmithing, with work of some leading jewelers, including Babetto, Sajet and Smit.

Galerie Lous Martin, Nieuwstraat 13, 2611 HK, Delft
Holland's latest addition to its thriving jewelry gallery network, directed by a pioneer of Dutch Modernist design.

Galerie Marzee, Ganzenheuvel 33, 6511 WD, Nijmegen
Well-known for promoting jewelry design in Holland. It presents installation projects and its new five-floor premises show photography, furniture and clothing design.

Galerie Ra, Vijzelstraat 80, 1017 HL, Amsterdam
Established in 1976, it has pioneered innovation in international jewelry.

Hans Appenzeller, Grimburgwal 1, 1012GA, Amsterdam
Also includes jewelry and product design by other makers.

Studio Ton Berends, Westeinde 22, 2512 HD, The Hague
Gallery space known for its sensitive arrangements of jewelry presentations.

EXHIBITIONS

Selected list of Dutch exhibitions published with catalogues.

1965 *International Jewellery*, Boymans Museum (organized by Hessisches Landesmuseum, Darmstadt)

1966 *Gijs Bakker and Emmy van Leersum*, Galerie Rietzje Swart, Amsterdam

1967 *Sieraad '67*, Galerie Het Kapelhuis, Amersfoort

1969 Opening exhibition, Galerie Sieraad, Amsterdam

1970 Group exhibition, Galerie Nouvelles Images, The Hague

1972 *Objects to Wear* (Gijs Bakker, Nicolaas van Beck, Françoise van den Bosch, Bernhard Lameris, Emmy van Leersum), Van Abbemuseum, Eindhoven and tour of USA

1972 *Sieraad 1900–1972*, Zonnehof, Amersfoort

1974 *56 Bracelets, 17 Rings, 2 Necklaces*, Visual Arts Office, Ministry of Culture, Amsterdam, European tour.

1978 *Françoise van den Bosch – Retrospective*, Stedelijk Museum, Amsterdam

1978 *British Jewellers on Tour*, Van Reekummuseum, Apeldoorn

1979 *Emmy van Leersum*, Stedelijk Museum, Amsterdam

1981 *VES*, Stedelijk Museum, Amsterdam

1982 *Marion Herbst, Overview 1969–1982*, Van Reekummuseum, Apeldoorn

1982 *Visies op Sieraden 1965–1982*, Stedelijk Museum, Amsterdam

1984 *Cross Currents: Jewelry from Britain, Germany, Holland and Australia*, Power House Museum, Sydney

1984 *Robert Smit*, Stedelijk Museum, Amsterdam

1985 *Images, 10th Anniversary VES*, Stedelijk Museum, Amsterdam

1986 *Sieraad 1986*, Draagteken, Museum Het Kruithuis, 's Hertogenbosch

1986 *10 Years Galerie Ra*, Galerie Ra, Amsterdam

1987 *Concept, Comments, Process, Dutch Jewelry 1967–87*, The Netherlands Office for Fine Arts, The Hague, European tour

1988 *London–Amsterdam: New Art Objects from Britain and Holland*, Galerie Ra, Amsterdam and Crafts Council, London

1989 *Gijs Bakker*, Centraal Museum, Utrecht

1990 *News from The Netherlands*, international tour of Dutch jewelry

1990 *American Dreams, American Extremes*, Museum Het Kruithuis, 's Hertogenbosch

1991 *Beauty is a Story*, Museum Het Kruithuis, 's Hertogenbosch

1991 *The Banqueting Table, 15 Years Galerie Ra*, Amsterdam

1991 *Ruudt Peters*, Galerie Marzee, Nijmegen

1993 *Facet 1*, Kunsthal, Rotterdam

1993 *Broken Lines, Emmy van Leersum – Retrospective*, Museum Het Kruithuis, 's Hertogenbosch, European and American tour

1993 *Manfred Bischoff*, Museum Het Kruithuis, 's Hertogenbosch

1993 *Marion Herbst, Works from 1968 to 1993*, Stedelijk Museum, Amsterdam

1994 *Daniel Kruger, Jewellery and Ceramics*, Museum Het Kruithuis, 's Hertogenbosch

1994 *Tekens en Ketens, Kussens en Kisten*, Museum Van Der Togt, Amstelveen

MAGAZINES

Bijvoorbeeld, Artforum Publishers, Hulkesteinseweg 16-a, 6812 DC, Arnhem

Items, Uitgeverij Bis, Noordeinde 19–21, 2611 KE, Delft

ITALY
PUBLIC MUSEUMS AND GALLERIES
There are well-known national collections of goldsmithing documenting Italian artists' past achievements but few, it seems, include 20th-century work. Consequently, major surveys and exhibitions are rare. The city of Padua plans to change this by building a permanent museum of jewelry on a par with Pforzheim.

Galleria Nazionale d'Arte Moderna, Viale Belle Arti 131 Rome

Large international collection of 20th-century painting, sculpture and jewelry.

PRIVATE

Galleria Adelphi, Via Giotto 4, Padua
Commercial gallery for contemporary fine art; since the 1960s, work by goldsmiths has formed part of their exhibition policy.

Studio GR20, Via dei Soncin 27, Padua
Contemporary jewelry exhibitions alongside collections of Art Deco.

Studio Marijke, Via Gabelli 7, Padua
Temporary exhibitions held intermittently with an emphasis on Dutch work.

EXHIBITIONS

1951 *IX Triennale*, Milan

1954 *Esempi di Decorazione Moderna di Tutto il Mondo*, Hoepli, Milan

1955 *Bruno Martinazzi*, Galleria Cairola, Milan

1955 *Mostra Nazionale di Oreficeria*, Venice

1959 *Martinazzi*, Galleria La Feluca, Rome

1962 *Salone Nazionale dell Oreficeria*, Venice

1963 *XIII Triennale*, Milan

1966 *Biennale d'Arte*, Venice

1970 *Biennale Internazionale d'Arte*, Premio del Fiorino, Florence

1977 *XI Biennale Internazionale*, Piccola Scultura, Padua

1979 *Triveneta delle Arte*, Villa Simes, Padua

1986 *Arte Moderna a Torino*, Palazzo della Promotrice di Belle Arte, Turin

1986 *Nine Goldsmiths from the School of Padua, XIV Biennale del Bronzetto*, Museo Civico, Padua

1987 *Giampaolo Babetto*, Galleria Stevens, Padua

1988 *Segnali per il Corpo*, Studio Pao, Milan

1989 *Anthology of Contemporary Goldsmith Art*, Studio GR20, Padua

1990 *Gioielli Legature, Artisti del XX Secolo*, Biblioteca Trivulziana, Milan

1991 *Rare Frazioni, Paolo Sardina, Graziano Visintin*, Galleria Civica, Padua

1995 *Mario Pinton – Retrospective*, Caff Pedrocchi, Padua

MAGAZINES

L'Orafo Italiano, Via Nervesa 6, Milan

Vogue Gioiello, Piazza Castello, Milan

Modo, Via Roma 21, Milan

BIBLIOGRAPHY

Arnason, H.H., *Calder*, Studio Vista-Van Nostrand, New Jersey, 1966

Black, Anderson, *A History of Jewels*, Orbis Publishing, London, 1974

Bodine, Sarah and Michael Dunas, *Jewelries/Epiphanies*, Artist Foundation Gallery, Boston, 1990

Boersma, Pieter & Gert Staal, *Sieraden op Straat*, Kunstschrift, Haarlem, Holland

Bott, Gerhard, *Schmuck*, Verlag Hans Schoner Konigsbach, Pforzheim, 1971

Bott, Gerhard et al., *Hermann Jünger, Schmuck nach 1945*, Germanisches Nationalmuseum, Nuremberg, 1988

Broadhead, Caroline, *New Traditions, The Evolution of Jewellery 1966–1985*, British Craft Centre, Contemporary Applied Arts, London, 1985

Cartlidge, Barbara, *20th Century Jewelry*, Harry N. Abrams, New York, 1985

Crawford, Alan, *C.R. Ashbee Architect, Designer and Romantic Socialist*, Yale University Press, New Haven and London, 1985

Crommelin, Liesbeth, *10 Years Galerie Ra*, Galerie Ra, Amsterdam, 1986

Crommelin, Liesbeth and Paul Derrez, *Rek in Het Sieraad*, Kunstschrift, Harlem, Holland, 19--

Den Besten, Liesbeth (ed.), *Concepts, Comments, Commentaries, Dutch Jewellery 1967–1987*, Netherlands Office of Fine Arts, The Hague, 1987

Dormer, Peter, *Design since 1945*, Thames and Hudson, London, 1993

Drutt, Helen, *Jewelry of our Time*, Thames and Hudson, London, 1995

Eidelberg, Martin (ed.), *Design 1935–1965, What Modern Was*, Musée des Arts Décoratifs, Montreal, 1991

Falk, Fritz, *Ornamenta 1*, Prestel Verlag, Munich, 1989

Farmer, David et al., *Design in America: The Cranbrook Vision*, Harry N. Abrams, New York, 1983

Fisch, Arline, *Textile Techniques in Metal*, Van Nostrand Reinhold, New York, 1975

Foley, Mark and Mark Isaacson, *Structure and Ornament, American Modernist Jewelry, 1940–1960*, 50 Fifty Gallery, New York, 1984

Fossati, Paolo et al., *Martinazzi*, Helen Drutt Gallery, New York, 1990

Getty, Nilda, *Contemporary Crafts of the Americas*, Henry Regnery Co, Chicago, 1975

Grant Lewin, Susan, *One of a Kind, American Art Jewelry Today*, Harry N. Abrams, New York, 1994

Grassetto, Folchini, Graziella, *Gioielli e Legatune Del XX Secolo*, L'Orafo Italiano, Editore, Padua, 1990

Herman, Lloyd, *Brilliant Stories, American Narrative Jewelry*, USA Information Agency, 1990

Heron, Susanna and David Ward, *The Jewellery Project*, Crafts Council, London, 1983

Hewison, Robert, *Future Tense, New Art for the Nineties*, Methuen, London, 1990

Hinks, Peter, *20th Century British Jewellery, 1900–1980*, Faber and Faber, London, 1983

Houston, John, *Caroline Broadhead: Jewellery in Studio*, Bellow Publishing, London, 1990

Hughes, Graham, *The Art of Jewelry*, Studio Vista, London, 1972

—, *Modern Jewelry*, Studio Vista, London, 1963

Jackson, Lesley, *The New Look Design in the Fifties*, Thames and Hudson, London, 1991

Kaplan, Wendy and Elizabeth Cumming, *The Art and Crafts Movement*, Thames & Hudson, London, 1991

Keisch, Christiane, *Renate Heintze, Schmuck*, Stekofoto, Halle, 1993

Künzli, Otto, *Providence Report*, Art Aurea, 3/1989, Ulm Donna

Lessor Wolf, Toni, *Arthur Smith, A Jeweler's Retrospective*, Jamaica Arts Center, New York, 1990

Lucie- Smith, Edward, *Albert Paley: Sculptural Adornment*, Renwick Gallery, Smithsonian Institution, Washington, 1991

—, *Art in the Seventies*, Phaidon, Oxford, 1980

MacCarthy, Fiona, *British Design since 1980*, Lund Humphries, London, 1982

—, *William Morris, A Life for our Time*, Faber and Faber, London, 1994

Manhart, Marcia and Thomas, *The Eloquent Object*, Philbrook Museum of Art, Tulsa, Oklahoma, 1989

Martin, Richard, *Fashion and Surrealism*, Thames & Hudson, London, 1989

Metcalf, Bruce, *On the Nature of Jewellery*, Crafts Council of Australia, Sydney, 1989

Metz, Tracy, *Facet 1*, Kunsthal, Rotterdam, 1993

Meyerowitz, Patricia, *Jewelry and Sculpture through Unit Construction*, Studio Vista, London, 1968

Morton, Philip, *Contemporary Jewelry, Craftsman's Handbook*, Holt, Rinehart & Winston, New York, 1994

Nordness, Lee, *Objects USA*, Thames and Hudson, London, 1970

Ober, Jerven, *Françoise van den Bosch (1944–1977)*, Françoise van den Bosch Foundation, Naarden, 1990

Polhemus, Ted, *Street Style*, Thames and Hudson, London, 1994

Richter, Andrea, *Schmuck Burg Giebichenstein 1970–1992*, Grassimuseum, Leipzig, Museum des Kunsthandwerks, 1993

Schollmayer, Karl, *Neuer Schmuck*, Verlag Ernst Wasmuth, Tubingen, 1974

Smith, Paul and Edward Lucie-Smith, *Craft Today, Poetry of the Physical*, American Crafts Museum, New York, 1986

Staal, Gert, *American Dreams, American Extremes*, Museum Het Kruithuis, 's Hertogenbosch, Holland, 1990

—, *Beauty is a Story*, Museum Het Kruithuis, 's Hertogenbosch, Holland, 1991

Staal, Gert et al., *Broken Lines, Emmy van Leersum*, Snoeck-Ducaju & Zoon, Gent, 1993

Talli Nencioni, Anny, *Giampaolo Babetto*, Aurum, Zurich, 1991

Talli Nencioni, Anny, *Robert Smit*, Aurum, Zurich, 1992

Turner, Ralph, *Contemporary Jewelry: A Critical Assessment 1945–75*, Studio Vista, London, 1976

Turner, Robert, *Four Artists Reflect*, Society of Art in Craft, Pittsburgh, 1991

Turner, Ralph and Peter Dormer, *The New Jewelry*, Thames and Hudson, London, 1985 and 1994

Uchida, Yoshiko, *Jewellery of Margaret de Patta*, The Oakland Museum, California, 1976

Van Berkum, Ans and Martijn van Oostsroom, *Marion Herbst, Retrospective*, Pictures Publishers, BV Wijk en Aalburg, Holland, 1993

Wardropper, Ian, 10 Goldsmiths, Rezac Gallery, Chicago, 1988

Watkins, David, *The Best of Contemporary Jewelry*, Batsford, London, 1994

Willcox, Donald, *Body Jewellery*, Pitmans, London, 1974

ACKNOWLEDGMENTS

Key: *l*=left, *r*=right, *c*=centre, *t*=top, *b*=bottom

© AGAGP, Paris, and DACS, London, 1996 35*r*; Collection American Crafts Museum, New York 12, 34*l*, 36*l* (Gift of Eugene Bielawski, 1976), 43*l* (Gift of the Johnson Wax Company from Objects USA, 1977. Donated to the American Crafts Museum by the American Craft Council); Archives of American Art, Smithsonian Institution 10*r*; The Board of Trustees of the Victoria and Albert Museum 14*c*, 16, 46*r*, 47*tr*, 47*br*, 57*r*, 71*t*; Collection Carrain, Italy 56*r*; Cleveland Contemporary Jewellery Collection, England 72, 111*r*; Crafts Council Collection 50*l*, 64*t*, 66, 67, 68, 111*l*, 114; © DACS 1996 54*bl*, 54*r*; Collection Deutsches Goldschmiedehaus, Hanau 58; Collection of Don and Heidi Endemann, Gualala, California 98; Collection Daphne Farago 41*l*, 120*r*; Collection Gem Montebello 23*t*, 24*t*, 24*b*, 54*tl*; Graber Collection, Switzerland 121; Courtesy Helen Drutt Gallery, Philadelphia 75, 97; Klaus Hansmann 60*l*; Hatch-Billops Collection, Archives of Black American Cultural History 10*l* (© Charles L. Russell), 10*c*; Minami Jewellery Museum, Kamakura, Japan. © DEMART PRO ARTE BV/DACS 1996 54 *cl*; Collection Minneapolis Museum of Art 43*r*; The Hiko Mizuno Collection, Tokyo 124; Musée des Arts Décoratifs, Montreal 33 (Liliane and David M. Steward Collection), 34*t*, 37 *tl*, 37 *bl*, 37*r*; Musée des arts décoratifs, Paris 107; Museum of Fine Arts, Boston. Gift of Mr and Mrs John Coolidge 35*l*; Collection Museum Het Kruithaus, 's Hertogenbosch 53*t*; Museum für Kunst und Gewerbe, Hamburg 19*b*; National Museum of American Art, Smithsonian Institution 40*b* (Gift of Mary Wadman), 48*b* (Gift of Helen Drutt Gallery and Falcon Press); Oakland Museum, Oakland, California 36*r* (Gift of Eugene Bielawski); Collection Dr Ron Porter, Columbia, South Carolina; Private Collection 23*c*, 59*r*, 126*tl*; Collection Gerd Rothmann 59*b* 78*b*, 101*b*; Collection Schmuckmuseum, Pforzheim 27*b*, 48*t*, 51*br*, 52*r*, 55*bl*, 55*r*, 59*t*, 61*tr*, 62, 63*t*, 71*bl*; Collection The Science Museum, London 70; Collection Shipley Art Gallery 64*b*; Courtesy Louise Smit Gallery 104; Collection Staatliche Museen, Berlin 20*b*; Collection Jo Stahr 101*t*; Collection Stedelijk Museum, Amsterdam 52*bl*, 52*r*, 69, 115*l*; Collection Ralph Turner 17*b*, 26*b*, 57*l*, 66; Collection The Worshipful Company of Goldsmiths 44*t*, 47*tl*, 49, 50*r*, 51*t*

PHOTOGRAPHERS

Ingrid Amslinger 20*t*; Rien Bazen 128; James Beards 73, 90; Karen Bell 91*t*, 91*b*, 95*t*; Ray Carpenter 67; Peter Chang 110; Pietro Chilesotti 54*r*; Donald Christie 122; Bob Cramp 70, 82; David Cripps 18*b*, 46*l*, 61*tl*, 61*b*, 109; CT Photostudio Leonburg 59 *br*; George Dobler 78*t*; M. Lee Fatherree 36*r*; Walter Fischer 19*t*; Andrew Forgoni 86*b*; Gavin Fraser-Williams 83; Pucci Gardina 23*c*; Markus Geldhauser 100*t*; Robert Goldman 77; Jochen Grün 103, 127*t*, 127*b*; Tom Haartsen 87; Mark Hamilton 49; Klaus Hansmann 60*l*; Thilo Härdtlein 99*tr*; Greg Heins 15*tl*; Eva Heyd 36*l*; Elisabeth Holder 79; Mark Johann 92; Peter Jones 15*tr*; Eva Jünger 126*r*; Ernst Jünger 19*b*; Richard Khoury 107 (inset); Otto Künzli 71*br*, 89*r*, 124, 125; Peter Mackertich 65, 64*b*; Thomas Manhart 44*b*; Bruno Martinazzi 126*bl*, 126*tl*; George Meister 56*l*; Gunther Meyer 27*t*; Bruce Miller 40*b*, 42, 45, 48*b*; Sara Morris 26*b*, 57*l*, 66, 111; Nina Mulas 24*b*, 54*tl*; Ugo Mulas 23*t*, 24*t*; Rigmor Mydtskou-Steen Ronne 12; D.P.P. Naish 47*tr*, 47*br*, 57*r*, 71*t*; Julian Nieman 17*t*; Wilfried Petzi 101*b*; Joel Pieper 75; Gary Pollmiller 38*l*, 38*tr*, 38*br*; Dean Powell 95*b*; Steve Pyke 88; Rampazzi 55*bl*; Giles Rivest 34*r*, 37*r*; Romeo Rolette 11; Bernhard Schaub 99*bl*, 99*br*; Gillesz Schippers 102; Philip Schönborn 29, 60*r*, 78*b*; Kirstin Schubaum 89*tl*, 89*bl*; Rik Sferra 97; Miriam Sharlin 14*r*; Mathys Shrofer 22; Coreen Simpson 10*tl*; Robert Smit 104; Eric Smith 31*t*; Robert Smith 53*b*; Janos Steckovics 112*l*, 112*r*, 113; Lorenzo Trento 80, 105, 107; Nick Turner 116*t*; Peter van der Kruis 52*bl*, 52*tl*, 53*t*; D. van der Meer 85; Het Vrije Volk 21*bl*; Cor van Weele 21*br*; Rob Versluys 118*b*; David Watkins (photocollage) 26*t*; Jasper Wiedeman 123*t*, 123*c*, 123*b*; Christoph Zellweger 114

INDEX

Page numbers in italic denote illustrations